I0490976

DROPSHIPPING

The Perfect Online Business Model with New Strategies to Generate Passive Income. Build a Successful E-commerce to Start Making Money Online and Achieve Financial Freedom.

Author Name: Harvey Quick

Table of Contents

Introduction

Congratulations on purchasing Book "Dropshipping" and thank you for doing so. This book will discuss extensively about dropshipping. There are hundreds of thousands of people who want to venture into the world of online business but do not have adequate information to turn their dreams into reality.

This book helps to demystify dropshipping as a model of doing business. Among the issues to be tackled in this book include:

- ➤ We will get to understand the dropshipping model of doing business. We will get to have a look at its benefits and also how this new model of doing business.
- ➤ We will have a look at what it takes to become an entrepreneur. Here we will focus on the mindset that a successful entrepreneur has and what they do differently from everyone else to ensure their success.
- ➤ We will have a look at the different strategies that you can use to adequately position your business

for success. Some of these strategies include the best marketing and SEO strategies, identifying how to leverage on the success of your business in order to scale it to greater heights.

➢ The strategies you can employ in order to find the right niche market and also the right products and suppliers for your start-up dropshipping business.

➢ We will have a look at some of the top e-commerce platforms and how we can use them as a home for our online business. These platforms are Shopify Amazon and eBay.

There are plenty of books on this subject on the market, thanks again for choosing this one! Every effort was made to ensure it is full of as much useful information as possible, please enjoy it!

Harvey Quick

November 20, 2019

Chapter 1: Understanding Dropshipping

Making money online has never been as easy as it is in these times we live in. About a decade or so ago, to have an online e-commerce business was an expensive affair to venture into. From expensive domain names and website hosting packages, to even higher website design and inventory costs, someone had to have a lot of startup capital to get things up and running. The rise of the dropshipping model of business came to clear all these hurdles, making it easier for investors and entrepreneurs to venture into the lucrative world of e-commerce.

Dropshipping can be defined as a fulfillment model that makes it possible for entrepreneurs and other online business owners to procure goods from a manufacturer or any other supplier who will in turn ship the product to your customer directly. This, therefore, eliminates the common or traditional mode of doing business whereas a business owner, you sell to your clients the stock that you have already purchased from the manufacturer or supplier. In the case of dropshipping, the product is shipped directly to your customer from the suppliers' storage unit.

Simply put, dropshipping enables you as a businessman to become a middleman or the connecting link between the manufacturer or supplier and the public you are selling to. This greatly reduces the risks involved in conducting business because you only need to find the right suppliers and market your online shop. All the logistical and inventory issues are handled by suppliers and manufacturers. After making a sale, the supplier deducts the costs they incur in the transaction, which are basically the cost of the product, shipping costs, and in some cases packaging costs, and then they send you the balance which is your profit. This, therefore, gives you the perfect opportunity to conduct business at minimal risk and cost.

Dropshipping is by no means a new phenomenon or scheme. It has always been in practice in one way or another, even years before the birth of the internet. Its popularity has been increasingly growing in the recent past because the internet makes it much more efficient and faster to conduct dropshipping transactions as the market is open to more people.

Dropshipping, How it Works

As we have already established, dropshipping is a method of conducting business whereas a businessman, you do not need to hold any stock in order for you to sell your products, but your suppliers will hold the stock on your behalf. Whenever an order is placed on your e-commerce website, the order together with the payment is delivered directly to the supplier of that particular product, who in turn delivers the product straight to your customer and sends you the profit you made in that transaction.

As the business owner, you will never get to see or handle the product, and neither will you process any payment at any point during the transaction. There, however, are some suppliers who will allow you to handle your own payments and even take care of all the shipping needs. Making such deals with your suppliers is counterproductive as it beats the goal of dropshipping.

There are quite a number of differences between the normal or traditional e-commerce mode of doing business and dropshipping. Let us take a moment to have a look at the major operational differences between the two.

1. **Margins:** An operating margin is a ratio that is used to determine the level of efficiency business is operating on and also its pricing strategy. The operating margin is used to measure the proportion of the company income that remains after it fulfills the variable operating overhead costs that it incurs. For a dropshipping company, the absence of inventory and storage costs tend to push down the operating margin as compared to that of a traditional e-commerce business.

2. **Logistics:** While running a normal e-commerce business, it has always been inevitable to avoid having some stock, or even having to deal with shipping logistics and expenses. For a dropshipping business, on the other hand, you do not have to handle those logistics and this, therefore, gives you the freedom to run your business from virtually anywhere. You will never have to worry about incurring storage, warehousing or any other inventory-related costs.

3. **Profit Velocity:** The hands-off nature of running a dropshipping e-commerce store has made this mode of doing business to become increasingly popular among upcoming e-commerce store owners. The reason why this is so is due to the

high-profit margins that are enjoyed by investors that venture this avenue. In business, it is always more profitable to sell products at a higher cost when you source them directly from the manufacturer.

4. **Entry Barriers:** These include the occurrence of premium business establishment costs and any other industry entry barriers that discourage entrepreneurs from venturing into online business. Businesses that have, however, adopted the dropshipping model of doing business are completely shielded from this. It is much easier and cheaper to start up and run a dropshipping business as compared to a normal e-commerce business.

The Mind-set of a Dropshipping Entrepreneur

To be a dropshipping entrepreneur you need to have a certain mindset in order to become a success in your niche market. Millions of people set up online businesses and e-commerce websites on an annual basis. A many of them fail, give up and quit u there are those few who tackle the hurdles and emerge as successful businessmen. Lack of proper preparation before embarking on the online business venture is more often than not the significant difference between successful and unsuccessful dropshippers.

There are a wide variety of reasons why people become entrepreneurs and venture into business. Nowadays, financial freedom is usually a popular reason as to why people will venture into business. An increasing number of people establish hobby businesses online while still at school and when they graduate, they simply turn their hobby business into their fulltime job.

A large majority of people usually opt to resign from their fulltime jobs to venture into online businesses. Whichever category you fall in, you should ask yourself one crucial question; "is this the right time to get started with this business venture?" This is a very important question as it helps you to evaluate yourself and our situation in order to help you fully determine whether or not you are up for the challenge. This question will help you determine the following factors among others in order for you to properly evaluate your level of preparedness for the task:

- Do I have enough capital to support starting up the venture?

- How will this venture blend in with my current day-to-day schedule?
- Am I ready to switch from a fulltime job to a part-time one?
- If you have a family, how well are they prepared for this and are they ready for it?
- If you have a product in mind, is there demand in the market for it?

All these are concerns are valid and may hold the key to the success of your venture. If you find yourself asking yourself these questions, you are on the right track as you are portraying signs of having the mindset of a dropshipping entrepreneur. Let us have a look at the mindset you need to have as a dropshipping entrepreneur in order to significantly increase your chances of dropshipping success.

No Looking Back

The number one driving force for many successful entrepreneurs is the necessity to make their dreams a reality but not just the desire to achieve it. This sense of urgency was the main driving force that pushed them to put in the extra effort in order to make their dreams come true. With this kind of a driving force, looking back is never an option. You should be willing to give your business your best in order for it to succeed. This means that even if you take a loan on your house in order to finance the business, such a decision should be a no-brainer because you know that you will do all it takes to make sure that your business is able to pay off such a loan.

Take a Reality Check

After deciding to break away from the norm and start a dropshipping business, there are a couple of factors that you will need to look at before you proceed. You will need to conduct intense market research, ensure you have enough cash to sustain the business and also your personal expenses, take time to discuss with your family regarding your decision and the impact of the business on your daily routine or schedule.

You need to have in mind that businesses do not immediately begin to rake in profits. It is important for you as the business owner to be very patient, determined, do not give up, and you should also be ready to make sacrifices so as to make sure that you will reap the benefits of your hard work when the time comes. You need to be ready to take on the responsibility that comes with owning a business. When things are not going as smoothly as they should, you are the final decision maker. Unlike being an employee, you do not have the luxury of sneaking out of work or clocking out exactly at 5 pm while the boss handles a chaotic state of affairs; you are the boss! If your only goal while venturing into the dropshipping world is just to make a quick profit, then chances are that you will not last very long as a business owner.

Your Own Merits and Demerits

It is next to impossible to find an all-rounded person that is an absolutely perfect businessman in that they possess all the necessary skills and expertise required in effectively running a business. It is perfectly natural for everyone to have their own strengths and weaknesses, and it is therefore important for you to understand this aspect of yourself as you are venturing into this business.

In order to achieve this, you will need to analyze your major accomplishments, both in your personal and professional life, as well as the skills you used to achieve them. Follow the steps below to help you perform this exercise.

1. **Make a Personal Resume.**

   A personal resume usually contains a list of the experience you have both professionally and personally as well as your experience. For each assignment, explain your duties and responsibilities, as well as your level of success. Make sure that you include your educational background, professional skills, personal interests (hobbies), and any achievement that needed any special knowledge or expertise.

2. **Analyze your Personal Attributes.**

This part of the exercise will enable you to reveal the things you like and hate or dislike, and also your weaknesses and strengths. This is important because it will help you identify the areas or business units that you will need to outsource or in the very least, get some help. For example, if you are not a people person, you may get someone else to handle the customer care functions of the business. In this case, you may also consider venturing to an industry that warrants minimal interaction with the customers.

3. **Analyze your Professional Attributes.**

As the entrepreneur of a small business, you do not need to become a jack-of-all-trades. In the areas that you are competent, perform those duties to your level best. In areas where you feel like you do not have the proper skills and expertise for, hire someone or outsource that particular function. It may be an expensive affair in the short run but eventually, when the business becomes profitable, you will reap the benefits of running your business professionally. To analyze your professional attributes, write down all the functions that will be required to be performed for the efficient running of your business. Alongside each function, note down your level of competence.

Define your Goals

It is important to properly define your business goals after analyzing our own strengths and weaknesses. The ultimate goal for venturing into business for some people is to have absolute freedom of their time and movement. Other people aim at achieving financial security.

Setting business goals is just as important as deciding the business you intend on venturing into. If you realize that your business does not meet your personal goals, you will be less motivated to put your effort into ensuring it grows.

When setting goals, you need to ensure that they have the following qualities so that they can work for you.

1. **Be Specific.**

   A goal is more achievable when it is specific as compared to a goal which is general. For instance, planning to kick off business by 1st November is more specific than planning to start operations sometime during the month of November.

2. **Be optimistic.**

   You will need to be positive-minded whenever you are setting your business goals. Planning to attain financial stability is a positive goal. Planning to be able to clear your bills on time is not.

3. **Be Realistic.**

   For goals to be achievable, they need to be realistic. If you fail to do this then you are destined to become a very frustrated businessman. For instance, it is more realistic to plan to increase your average monthly sales by 10% than planning to earn a profit of $100,000 in the first month of operations.

4. **Have a clear distinction between the Short-term and Long-term Goals.**

   It is important to have a very clear distinction between short-term goals and long-term goals in order for you to be able to set realistic goals. Short-term goals are those that are achievable within 12 months while long-term goals can only be achieved over a long duration of more than 12 months. In our previous example, increasing average monthly sales by 10% is a short-term goal while earning a monthly profit of $100,000 is a long-term goal.

Factors to consider when setting goals

1. **Level of Income.**

   Given that many entrepreneurs venture into business in order to attain financial stability, it is important for you to plan how much money you want to make in your first year of operations, and the years that follow. This plan should cover the first 5 years of operations.

2. **Kind of Work.**

   You need to determine the kind of work and the working conditions that you are most comfortable with as you set the goals for the kind of work.

3. **Lifestyle.**

   This focusses on certain aspects of your work conditions such as working hours, travel and business location. It will address issues such as your working hours, location and also use of the personal property for business purposes.

4. The gratification of Self Ego.

Being a business owner comes with it some form of status and glamour. It is no wonder it is not a surprise that you will find many entrepreneurs who got into business simply to gratify their own egos. It is therefore important for you to decide on how important gratifying your ego is to you and venture into the kind of business that fulfills that desire.

Tapping into the Right Niche Market

A niche market can be defined as a particular subgroup of a much broader market where customers who have a particular set of needs or problem(s) can be found. For instance, we have the clothing industry which is massive and has many major players who are in competition with each other. As a small business owner, you may lack the proper resources to compete at a level playing field.

At this point, you need to filter out the fashion categories you are not interested in and address a much smaller and specific market segment, like clothes for children. Once you have identified this, dig deeper and further reexamine this subgroup and identify a much better niche that you will be comfortable operating in. An example of a niche within the subgroup 'clothes for children' would be clothes for children aged below 3 years. Now, this would be identified as your niche market.

The deeper you dig into a market segment and focus on a smaller, more specific segment of the market, the higher your chances of success will be. Always make an effort to dig as much as you can in order to find the right trading environment for your business.

What Makes a Good Niche Market

For marketing purposes, there are basically 2 different types of niche markets.

1. Niche markets where people have extreme issues that require an immediate solution. E.g. health industry.
2. Niche markets where people have a passion and derive pleasure from engaging in it. E.g. hobbies.

When people have serious issues, desperation will send them looking for an urgent solution and if you are able to provide it, then they will do anything to get it from you. This is the main reason why industries such as health, weight loss, and other personal problems such as quick get-rich businesses and online dating are such profitable industries.

People are also more likely to spend a lot of money on things that they are passionate about and/or give them pleasure. This is simply because they always feel good about it. This is the reason why industries such as beauty and sports are also profitable markets.

It is also important to consider other aspects such as the size of the market, demand for the commodity, product availability, and whether or not the niche market you have identified is seasonal or not.

Finding a Niche Market

For many people who venture into an online business, the common belief is that you need to figure out a product or something that no one else has discovered or at the very least, a product that does not have a lot of competition among other markets. The truth, however, is that there is no niche that is unknown to marketers but it is only unknown to you.

There is a chance that you may find a niche that is not being marketed actively but high chances are that there is a pretty good reason for that. In most cases, the reason for this is that the niche does not have enough demand or there is no money to be made there.

The main thing you need to realize is that you need to go after those niche markets that are evergreen, have customers, demand and products on sale and also a proven history of being marketable. And as you do this, always remember to go for those sub-niche markets where you feel comfortable trading in.

Let us now have a look at some of the factors you need to consider when you are finding your perfect niche.

Analyze your Problems and Likes

As we saw in the previous section of an Entrepreneurs' mind-set, you need to evaluate your personal interests in order to identify whether or not you are ready to start up a business. This case also applies when you are hunting for your ideal niche market.

It is important for you to look for a niche market that you are knowledgeable about or have a genuine interest in. To identify this, you need to grab a pen and a notebook and write down the problems you may have in your daily life, health, finance, and the normal challenges that you face on a daily basis. In a nutshell, note down anything and everything that you may be interested in creating your online product or project around. This exercise is more of a brainstorming session where you are simply trying to come up with ideas. You, therefore, do not need to analyze these ideas in terms of profitability.

With your ideas, notebook, and pen, you need to start analyzing these ideas from a marketing point of view. You will be baffled by the number of niche ideas that you may come up with by taking this perspective. Make sure you always carry your pen and notebook so that you can always note down any material you may pick up along the way regarding your ideas. Be it from conversations with friends and family, from print media, television, radio, adverts, and the list is virtually endless. By the end of the day, you should have a healthy list of niche market ideas.

Analyze Current Trends

You may have analyzed your interests and realized they cannot be monetized. Do not worry, you can simply follow the money by looking at the current and future trends in order to find your ideal niche market. You may turn to the following online sources to help you get a better understanding of the trending consumer and market trends.

1. Amazon.com

This is one of the biggest e-commerce platforms in the world. As a shopper, you can buy almost anything under the sun from this website. The products on this online marketplace range from clothes, computers, car parts, boats, you name it. This, therefore, makes it one of the best sources you may use to discover amazing niche markets.

Going about this is pretty simple. You just need to reveal a list of categories or niches by clicking on the 'Departments tab that is located below the main search bar. This reveals a drop-down menu with a list of niche markets and when you click on any nice, you will be taken to a new page that contains a list of all the sub-niche markets (sub-categories) under that niche.

When you select on any sub-niche, you will be taken to another page that has further refined that sub-niche into several other sub-niche markets, and so on. Repeat this process until you find a niche that is right for you. You can try it out by visiting https://amazon.com. For example, if you want to enter the automotive industry, your niche selection on Amazon.com would be something similar to the chain shown below:

Automotive (main niche market) > Motorcycle and Powersports > Parts > Engine > Clutches.

On Amazon.com, it will look as shown below:

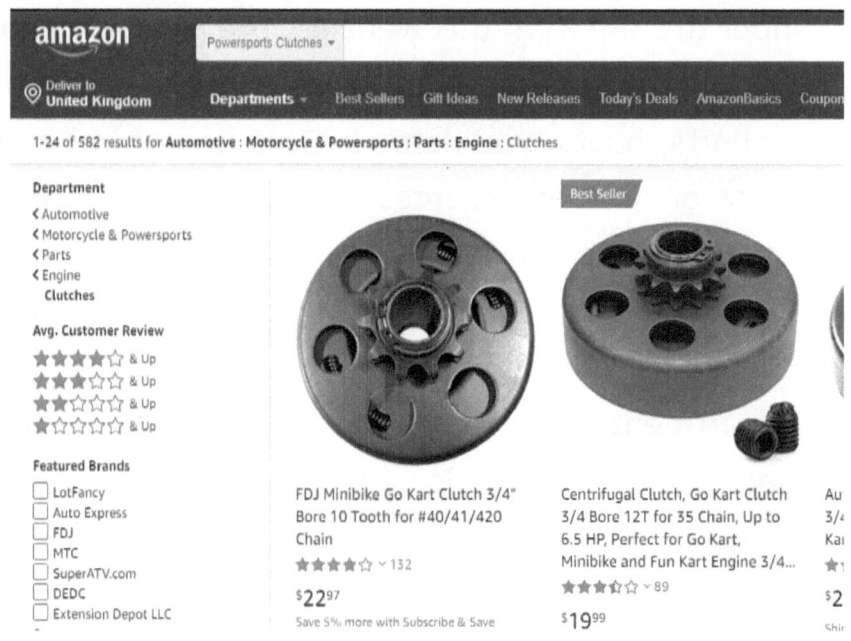

If you are going for the money and selling the goods that are currently trending or being bought the most, you can have a look at their best seller section that you can access using the 'Best Seller' tab which is right next to the 'Department" tab.

2. Google Trends

Google Trends is a product launched by Google that gives information regarding the popular and trending searches online. You can use this tool to identify which niche markets people are searching for online. This tool has many amazing features including ability to compare more than two keywords/products, you can localize the keyword or product search by country and in some countries, you can redefine your search further by city or state. It even gives you the other popular search term variants that people use. For some products, Google Trends also give an anticipated future trend of your desired product. You can access it by visiting https://trends.google.com/trends/. The picture below shows a simple search where we compare iPhone and Samsung keyword searches in the United States.

3. Clickbank.com

This is the world's leading digital marketplace. You can very simply compare it to amazon.com when it comes to digital products. Just like Amazon, Clickbank has a very professional categorization of its niche markets into smaller sub-niche markets.

To access it, just visit their website on www.clickbank.com and on the left-hand side of almost every page of their website, you will see the categories section. Here you will see the main categories, or niche markets, and when you click on the plus sign and you will reveal the sub-niche markets in every top-level niche market. Select the sub-niche market of your choosing and here you will get to see the products being offered in this particular sub-niche. This may help you in getting a few product ideas and if there are many products in any particular niche or sub-niche, it is a positive indicator of a profitable market.

Brand Oriented Marketing versus Product Oriented Marketing

Product Oriented Marketing

Product-oriented marketing is the process in which a product is introduced to the market and consequently overseeing its general success. The main areas where the product marketers focus on are understanding the customer base and marketing the product to them. They promote the market demand and usage of the product in the form of writing positioning and messaging. The main duty lies at the point where marketing and sales of the product intersect, meaning it can be quite difficult to define.

What Product Marketers Engage in

Before a product is launched, the marketers will basically take charge of the product positioning, collecting market feedback, and generally go through the product's marketing strategy. After the product is launched, assistance is provided to the sales team by the marketing team to ensure that sales are promoted and it is focussed on driving the demand of the product, general market acceptance, and overall product success.

Functions of Product Oriented Marketing

Every professional and successful product marketer knows that at the heart of every campaign strategy is the knowledge and a proper understanding of your client base. This ensures that:

- ➢ The product and its new unique features are properly positioned in the market.
- ➢ Ensuring that the respective teams in the sales and marketing departments have the necessary knowledge that will ensure they are able to bring in new clients.
- ➢ There is a steady increase in the acceptance and demand for the product in the market.
- ➢ The product has the capability to cater to a particular clientele need, one that a majority of similar products available in the market cannot satisfy.
- ➢ As the market changes and trends evolve, the product will be positioned in such a way that it remains relevant.

Product Oriented Marketing Deliverables

In business, whatever cannot be measured is not worth pursuing, it is, therefore, important for every product marketer to have a list of deliverables. Some of these deliverables include the following:

- ➢ The personas of the clients which provide the company with invaluable insights data.
- ➢ Attracting prospective clients and converting them into leads by proper brand positioning and communication.
- ➢ Supporting the sales team to land more clients by providing them with the right sales promotional materials.
- ➢ A primary marketing strategic plan that properly indicates how the product will be launched and marketed.

Brand Oriented Marketing

As opposed to product-oriented marketing, brand-oriented marketing is a method that highpoints the brand whenever a product or service is marketed. The main aim of brand-oriented marketing is linking your individuality, values, and personality with communicating with your audience. Your rand basically acts as a bridge between your clientele and the product.

Brand oriented marketing is not just about placing your company name and logo in as many places as possible and expect to generate sales. Because of the long duration of time it takes, many people usually tend to downplay the importance of brand-oriented marketing. The effect of this is having many marketers stuck on achieving short-term goals rather than placing more efforts in growing long-term goals such as growing the brand. Long-term goals are much more beneficial to the company as a whole.

Importance of Developing Strategic and Consistent Brand Equity

In order to grow your business's level of trust, reputation and market reach, it would be very advantageous if you also grow your brand. The ultimate result of this is that your products will have a higher market value. BMW is a good example of a business that has brand equity which will last well into the future. It hs grown a genuine brand by positioning itself as an innovation guru in the industry. The brand's main focus is on the quality of their cars, with a key emphasis on the safety of the people inside.

How to Create a Branding Strategy that is Best Suited for your Business

It is very crucial for you to formulate a long-term plan whenever you embark on growing a brand. The following four factors determining how your marketing strategy will be shaped.

1. Formulation of a company vision
2. Determination of a target audience
3. Consistency
4. Communicating emotion

Company Vision Formulation

You should first decide on what you want your company to be known for, then come up with a strategy to convey that message through all the available channels of communication. For example, choose whether you want your business to be known for its innovation (like Apple) for promoting joy and happiness (like Coca-cola).

Determination of a target audience

You could end up conducting an unsuccessful brand marketing campaign if you choose not to identify a target audience. A targeted case here means more than just a mere understanding of the demographics. On the contrary, a target market should be segmented further and broken down into psychographics and clarified y creating procuring personas.

Be Consistent

The manner in which you interact with your clients over time is an important cornerstone of effective brand marketing. The message, sounds and visual aesthetics, and rand tone should be recognized easily and aligned for the long-term. Consistency promotes trust and loyalty.

Communicating Emotion

The brand at Coca-Cola is based on an emotional relationship with its customers. You'll have entered into the complete potential of brand marketing and the benefits in the long term if you place your company as a must-have brand. Do not care about establishing mental connections other than with the world's largest marketing budget. Zappo clients have established an emotional link with the brand by offering excellent customer service and by offering randomly unexpected clients with next day delivery. Zappos is known to go beyond and beyond its clients, from ordering clients to deliver a free couple of shoes to a shoot less and finest marriage person. Zappos has therefore established an emotional relationship with its clients, which creates allegiance that contributes to repeated shopping and promotion.

Ensure your Brand Follows through in real life

You could have the greatest brand in character, layout, content, and consistency, but all these attempts might be wasted if your item does not keep its commitments to its clients. When trying to create a solid brand, product quality should be the main consideration. If you have a bad quality of item or service, it badly impacts your brand perception. Moreover, you should guarantee that quality coverage covers all fields of the company's customer communication — including social media platforms and help.

Choosing the Best Marketing Strategy

More than 150 marketing policies are in place. There is a multitude of marketing strategies from traditional to mobile to social, and you likely have attempted a lot. But do you choose the correct instruments? Your marketing strategy relies on your marketing objectives, target groups, character, budget, place, etc.

Determine your Marketing Goal

There's also some advice to find out what's going to be good for you before you jump into this range and begin to randomly try them. The choice of the most effective advertising approach begins with the definition of a defined objective. What is your marketing objective? Is it intended to increase brand awareness, enhance lead generation or increase direct sales? Answering these issues will assist you in determining which methods you want.

Determine the Target Market

You must always be at the heart of your prospective clients. Who do you speak to? Determine the best methods to communicate with your clients, including detecting your desired routes for interaction and buying routes. Where and when your target audiences are supplemented with the marketing strategies you choose. Note: certain businesses begin to believe that their goal is one community, only to discover another crowd that shows interest. Don't worry about changing gears.

Set up a budget for marketing

A company with two staff will have a marketing budget that is very distinct from a global company. But both have to spend money on spreading the term every year. Some of those 150 approaches will be eliminated and others will become more attractive with your budget. You can add strategies or boost the instruments that you use when you develop and your marketing budget rises.

Do you need assistance? Read how your marketing budget can be created.

Location

The mantra of the real estate market is the location, the location, the position, and the place. You will approach Pay Per Click, for instance, differently from a Raleigh attorney seeking customers within a 10-mile radius if you are a nationwide business. In addition, in some geographical places, certain methods operate better than others.

Take your sector into consideration

Advocates and dental professionals still use direct mail to achieve prospective clients. This approach operates for them as individuals often choose a local dentist and a lawyer only when they need one (for instance after an incident). Direct mail often operates for home facilities, but snail mail may not be a worthwhile location to invest your cash if you are a free photographer, too.

Choose Wisely

Although you can execute as many marketing strategies as you can, this is not the wisest choice. In addition to the elevated price, you can strive to see what approaches are functioning and what cash is wasted.

Marketing is something which should by its very nature be repeated and continuously implemented in order to be efficient. Sales and brand awareness can be generated by choosing the correct marketing actions.

Best SEO Strategies

There are four primary areas that an online business owner needs to consider as he is developing the business's SEO strategies. They are the pillars that form the foundation of a winning SEO strategy.

Technical SEO

Technical SEO can appear a bit daunting, but it is really about ensuring a search engine can read and view your content. The content management scheme you use is responsible for much of this and instruments such as Screaming Frog and Deep Crawl can discover your site and address technical issues.

On-site SEO Optimization

Your website should be optimized at the entire stage of each page. There is a crossover from your technical headquarters, and you would like to begin with a sizeable content hierarchy for your website. If you have a well-structured location, it is again comparatively easy to use reasonable optimization. Take time to consider your clients when you optimize your location. If you are a local company, local SEOs are more essential and your place and email become key optimization points. Layering your optimization on-page with a strong technical SEO in location is simple. Using instruments such as Screaming Frog, weaknesses can be identified and your websites methodically operate.

Content

Content is king. This is the saying, correct? This is the saying. In a manner, it is real. Your website is just a content wrapper. Your content informs you of what you are doing, where you are doing it, who you did it for and why someone should use your company. And if you are clever, your material should also go beyond the evident components of the brochure and assist your potential clients to attain their objectives. It is very essential to understand that SEO is essential for all such material, but that it is often only really taken into account in terms of service content. In confidence material, such as assessments, evidence, and case studies, SEO is often overlooked.

Off-site SEO

All SEO streams will finally reach one location: the building of power. In a big portion, constructing your power includes construction links. Connections are still a key element in the development of powerful organic rankings; however, connections can be SEO's hardest part to correct.

It really is essential to dial your connected philosophy before you begin, as this can really do your connecting attempts or split them up. While connection construction is a profound topic we can't address in detail here, you are already ahead of the bulk of your competition if you can at least create a favorable concept of link building:

- Make sure that you create the true connections which make sense in the actual globe and do not disturb the algorithms' qualitative and sometimes punitive components.
- Ensure that you have material to rank with which you want to link.

Web Traffic

Is it popular? It's certainly lovely to notice and everything, but is this the point? In order to praise and say, yes... I had 1.000.000 visitors last year on my site... maybe it's awesome, but why does website traffic matter to your company?

Traffic in the database (or amount of visitors) is essential because the amount of visitors corresponds to the number of fresh customer possibilities. The amount of visitors to your page makes your company the best of possibilities to communicate their brand, make an idea, create relationships. The more traffic on your Website, the greater the chances of generating skilled leads, fostering and helping to fix its issue and eventually selling your item or service, gaining a fresh client and growing your company continuously.

It's not just money-making. More ongoing internet traffic can help you (not only your profit) grow your company, expand your product lines, recruit more people, open fresh places, invest in studies and create more incredible products and facilities... there are more possibilities here!

The flow of your website is essential and has an effect in three respects: the higher the number of visitors! But, because not everyone traffic is excellent traffic, concentrate on enhancing the value of your blog. Bad traffic could actually hamper your company somewhat. As you boost your traffic and visitors ' value, the more you can boost the transformation of your site and make it paying clients!

How much traffic on the internet does your company need to grow?

All right, you mean, send me the digits. This is an easy but advanced calculation. You need to know the cost and expenditure of your company and the value of a mean client. You can then revert to the amount of income (specifying targets) you need to calculate the amount of website traffic to achieve that objective. Basically, you are looking back at your ultimate objective and planning.

Example: Your "cupcake business" has started and run. To keep your present budget, your company requires $5,000 a month. The value of each client is 30 $(usually 12 cupcakes per month are purchased at 2.50). 2.000 cupcakes must be sold a month. On average every client purchases 12 cupcakes a month, so every month you need 166,66 clients.

On a small average... 100 visitors to the page convert to 1 lead. At a conversion rate of 1 percent from a client, 100 leads will be needed to get one fresh client. It appears that you need to attract 1,666,666 visitors to your 166.66 clients' target. Phew, it appears as much as a job.

Please note that the small 1 percent transformation proportion is a conserving basis, but companies using inbound marketing strategies and other internet tactics see their conversion levels boost. You have only reduced your complete site traffic to 208,325 with a conversion rate of 2 percent and your client rates of 4 percent with stronger traffic and leads. This is 87.5% Wow reduction! It goes without saying that website traffic is not the only thing your company requires and that you have to maintain this in mind based on your sector and market. However, your website may play a major role in the achievement of your business!

You can also improve your transformation amount when you are able to boost website traffic and visits to your internet, which in turn reduces the number of fresh blog visitors you need to meet your company targets. Bearing in mind that the complete amount of visitors is not always important, but that they are interested and willing to purchase. The more sales channel your internet visitors are interested in your alternative or item, the more likely you are to boost the transformation.

The other major element of the website traffic equation is your ability to catch and transform the focused traffic on the website into clients. Inbound marketing may be just what your company requires if you are prepared to catch present website traffic and boost your skills!

Upselling Strategies

Upselling is the process where business owners will encourage their customers to make an additional purchase to the first one hence making the initial purchase more expensive. This happens during the same transaction. A good example is when you are trying to bronze a subscription package and the web system tries to convince you to upgrade your membership to a more expensive silver package. Below are a few upselling strategies you can use to boost your sales.

Take the time to see what achievement will mean to them.

You must know clearly what kind of achievement is essential to your customers before you can try to offer extra importance to your customers. You should put aside time to lay down early in your partnership and talk about what your client wishes to get from using your item or service. Discover the short term objectives and the larger, long-term plans of the customer as well.

To build confidence from the beginning, it is essential to develop a profound knowledge of the priorities of your clients. You can recognize where extra goods and facilities can assist you down the line if you understand what your customers' value and where they want to go.

Set measurable targets and monitor them.

Make sure you agree on clear and measured indices of achievement in working together using your item or service when you embark on a fresh client. Make use of what you know about the objectives and objectives of your clients and create an action plan with milestones to follow up on their advancement. For a need for additional service to be identified in the future of the customer, you need a means of recognizing areas where the existing game plan is short or where it can afford to improve the results of their resources. Careful follow-up is crucial in this respect.

You'd better have the information to back up if you inform a client that he requires more to spend on social media ads. As far as upselling is concerned, information is used to add to your discussion, and to show the client that it cares best.

Identify clients for whom extra services are really required.

Not every client is a good fit for upselling and never tries to push somebody who doesn't really need them with extra products or facilities. Generally speaking, it is not worth selling if you can't clarify how the extra buy benefits the customer's overall targets.

For instance, you shouldn't force email marketing to pitch your customer in an additional email marketing upgrade, but your email marketing doesn't match straight into your long-term plans for broadening your scope. You risk causing significant harm to the partnership, possibly losing its company if you attempt to sell products that have a small opportunity of producing a positive result.

Concentrate your improvement attempts instead of clients with a clear gap in their present strategy. If a client wants to extend its reach but doesn't believe they are moving in the correct direction, there is likely a chance for her to purchase an upgrade.

Begin to provide importance with fast victories as quickly as feasible.

No one will spend any extra funds in your company until you have demonstrated that it can produce concrete outcomes for your company. You should concentrate on making fast gains sooner rather than later in order to establish a lengthy, mutually profitable connection with a client.

A fast victory is anything that provides a client with instant importance. A check of the current social media strategy, an assessment of the customer's website to recognize fresh optimization possibilities, or even to develop a product offering, as well as a straightforward marketing plan could be a few instances.

If you make a fast gain, you don't need to make a big effort. It just has to prove your commitment to bring your client true yields from day one–and you can assist with your goods or facilities. The earlier you demonstrate measurable achievement to your customers, the earlier you can deepen the connection and demonstrate your knowledge in other fields.

Ideas for pitch— not upgrades only.

The reason why you believe an extra acquisition is a good idea needs to be fully understood. If you come to her and say, "I believe you have to invest more on social media," she could take the incorrect concept and conclude that you are only attempting to line yourself up.

Take a new upgrade in the context of an idea always. You should come up with a real plan for helping a client boost their returns from email marketing. Don't just say that she wants to invest more— offer her a well-understood scheme to see where her cash is invested and how this will help her general achievement through an upgrade.

Time is boosting with milestones.

It may be difficult to find the perfect time to contact a client on extra facilities and products. Following the completion of a successful product initiative or a major milestone (for instance, reaching a new leading target) take the opportunity to step back and ask your client, "What's next?" Talks about the future provide the opportunity to develop new ideas and projects with your client. Pitching an upsell is particularly efficient after you help your customers to make a large victory since they have evidence of their knowledge.

Enter a price breakdown that is clear.

For a time, put yourself in the hands of your clients: you would likely not bite if anyone said you had to give them more cash for slightly specified extra advantages. Actually, you might think that they are attempting to use you.

It is particularly essential that transparent sales data is provided if you propose an upsell. Give your client a full overview of your suggestions and clarify the costs and time required carefully. If a client understands where their hard-earned funds are heading, it is better to invest more cash in your products. (But if you are not comfortable raising the cost, your customers could have a nice chance to talk to your team's marketing representative.)

Identify patterns for your sales process and use them.

Once you have sold a few clients effectively, you will get a clearer concept of what clients are the most benefiting of extra products. Follow the timing and characteristics of these clients and integrate developments in your sales process to define upsales on a permanent basis proactively.

To persuade them, use social evidence.

Before creating large and costly buy choices, most individuals need proof to persuade them. That's the logic behind the client reviews value after all. Make certain that you have the information and proof to help you out from other clients or reviews with an add-on item before calling to persuade your client of an upsell.

For example, if you know how many customers in addition to the product already purchased by the customer introduced are used for the additional product, please inform them. If your business has obtained felicitous clients ' feedback using the extra item, inform them.

Leveraging on your Positive Trend

You can make use of leverage as an extremely strong asset in your company. Businessmen often say, "If you want to have accomplished something correctly... do it yourself." Only if you are willing to do it yourself, because you are a specialist or because you have time and means to do it. Intelligent entrepreneurs will nevertheless discover methods to use other individuals ' abilities, capabilities, time and money to do so better than they themselves or to optimize effectiveness. There is simply an unwise number of work to be done in such a short period that some help can pay dividends in the long term. If you have someone to assist you with a job, so that you can concentrate more time on stuff you are a specialist, your company will immediately enhance. There's a steady discussion between "work hard" and "working intelligent," which ultimately brings you further than you ever were. It is highly important to operate smartly in start-ups or as entrepreneurs because you would like to get the most out of every minute of work done.

Businessmen just have to do more with less. It is also essential to be difficult at work, but you get the most from all you do when you mix hard work with smart work. In company, it's all about constructing partnerships with individuals and treating them as real individuals rather than just throwing your item off your flesh. It's a two-sided advantage for both sides when using leverage. In this context, just because you can, you should never benefit from anyone. Everything is about ethics.

We have already discussed how to use leverage previously in blogging for traffic. The two types of leverages are strategies such as client reporting and relations with influencers. You benefit from their existing crowd and receive precious material for your readers. Groove, the startup "assist desk" internet assistance scheme, used its readers. Groove, the online help desk system startup, uses leverage to increase people's consciousness by tapping into a new company, Buffer. They achieved tremendous visibility in a brief spell as they were prepared to publish on the Buffer blog. In one article, Groove had over two or even three visitors to its e-mail list on its own blog in combination.

The greatest businessmen can do more with fewer than others in networking and networking. Networking is a strong instrument but it contains a fine line. Do it properly, and the funds accessible to you will make yourself more effective than ever before. Do it badly and you will only have poor relations. It's terrible.

 Think of networking as a friend. "It takes you long to have the correct way to think that networking makes friends. Don't you like a bit of meat treating your buddies? All about regard for one another is a partnership. Ideas are the best thing that you can offer.

Don't offer and you're going to earn. Nothing in exchange ever to fear. A connection can be constructed on the knowledge exchange, which ultimately helps everyone. When offering someone precious thoughts. Having friends is the moral of the tale!

Besides types of leverage for constructing relations and exposure gains, there is another way to make use of leverage to enhance your company's effectiveness. This is because we understand that there are too many assignments and not enough time to be accomplished. Even if a person in the nature of start-up building or being an entrepreneur can't do this all by themselves with incredible priority skill. You need assistance. You must discover someone more capable of doing the work than you or someone to assist them saves time exponentially. One excellent way of finding assistance is to discover free individuals who are prepared to provide their abilities, time and money in return for compensation or some kind of refund. In contrast to a full-time worker, the cost of recruiting freelancers is lower. Freelancers are not receiving health advantages, dental advantages or other advantages. As a startup, it is worth recalling that your cash flow is tremendously saved while still being supported by skilled freelancers.

This might be surprising, but Uber drivers are not Uber's full-time workers. Uber argues their drivers are recruited as self-employed. Uber, now a multi-national startup company, is recruiting its drivers as freelancers using a distinct type of business model. This allows them to function in the nature of their items. You must not care about maintaining them this way, because you have freelancers. You don't have to worry about keeping freelancers after the project is completed because they will then move to another project because being freelancers. But freelancers always think that working for a particular company fits them well and want to become long-term associates. If a company succeeds, it will ultimately recruit full-time workers. It's a fantastic indication! Regardless of whether you are an independent or a worker, always honor them. One of my favorite ideas is to treat the gardener with the same regard as the CEO. Using leverage means doing more with less, working cleverly AND working hard and making friends.

Chapter 2: Shopify

This is one of the largest e-commerce websites available on the internet. It has a particular section of their online platform that is solely dedicated to dropshipping. One of the main advantages of using Shopify is its simplicity in usage. Using Shopify, you can open an account and create a dropshipping store in well under 30 minutes. Once you have created it, Shopify has provided you with a wide range of tools to help you customize your store to suit its intended purpose. These tools include a custom domain name purchasing tool, supplier and product sourcing tools, payment gateways, customer support tools, and so much more.

The Shopify platform has an e-commerce module that is unique only to this platform and it offers business owners with a wide range of payment modes and options. This is a huge plus to you as a business owner because you will be able to provide these options to your customers and reduce your chances of losing customers due to issues like the inability to make a payment.

The Shopify e-commerce platform has been in existence for quite some time now and it provides you with all the tools you need to get started with your online dropshipping business venture.

Amazon merchants usually prefer Shopify as a trading platform, simply because of its simplicity in usage and professional functionality. It enables a business owner to completely customize their store to fully represent their unique brand. This saves you from looking the same as the other hundreds of thousands of e-commerce websites that are available online.

In this chapter, we will have a look at how to get your online dropshipping business up and running and have you ready to make some money in less than a day.

Setting up your Store

In this section of the chapter, we will have a look at the steps that you need to take so as to get your store set up.

As we have already noted Shopify is an easy to use e-commerce platform. It is one of the largest e-commerce platforms available and has been in existence for a long time and therefore they enjoy certain benefits or economies of scale.

Opening an account is easy. Once you visit their website on https://shopify.com, you will see a textbox prompting you to enter your email. Once you complete the registration process, you will be prompted to choose a premium package and enter your credit card details. One of the benefits of operating a Shopify store is that they give you access to their premium services for free. This gives you the chance as an entrepreneur to test out their systems, sourcing for products and suppliers and identify whether Shopify is the right platform for your business needs. You can, therefore, skip the premium package selection step of the registration process and go straight to the "Admin Section" of your shop.

You need to know that Shopify only gives a 14 day free access period for every account so you better make the best use of this time and learn the ins and outs of setting up and running the business. Once this period lapses, you will have to select a premium package in order to access any section of your website. Your content is never deleted from the database so you need not worry about losing anything.

Choosing a plan
The first issue people concern themselves with whenever they are opening a Shopify shop is the cost implications

of running one. Well, the Shopify Team understand that you may not be sure as to whether or not you want to build your dropshipping business completely on its platform, and thus as we have already established, they offer you a 14 day trial period in which all of the necessary instruments for the set-up of a good dropshipping shop are fully accessible. You will have to subscribe to a payment plan after this period is expired. The basic Shopify package, which comes up to $29 per month; Shopify package, which comes up to $79 each month; and Advanced Shopify package which comes down to $299 per month, are basically the three main three subscriptions plans offered by Shopify.

When you startup, it's safe to subscribe to the cheapest subscription plan, but it's better for you to upgrade your package as your revenues increase. So this raises the issue of when it is time to update your subscription to a better and more expensive one? Whenever you receive big orders a month, like more than 100 orders a month, it is high time for you to upgrade your plan to from the Basic Shopify package o the Shopify package, as your clients benefit from reduced credit card fees. You will also get more worker slots in order to enable you to recruit more employees who will help you handle your growing customer base.

In contrast to the Basic Shopify package plan, the Shopify package gives you access to and use the abandoned cart recovery tool, since it can validate the increased monthly fee incurred in order to receive your customers or orders. You can of course download and use third-party applications for this purpose, but the abandoned cart retrieval tool from Shopify has the best performance.

Setting up your domain Name

The next stage is to choose a nice domain name that correctly represents your business after choosing a payment plan with which you are satisfied with. The team at Shopify is kind enough to give your shop a free domain name, i.e. yourbusinessnam.myShopify.com, but the use of this free domain name should not be recommended. This is primarily because it portrays both you and your company as highly unprofessional. Moreover, as far as internet conversions and SEO ratings are concerned, as Google and other search engines do not preferably rate domain names under the domain name of myShopify.com.

Therefore, you must purchase a domain name tailored to your company first when you effectively activate your online store. There are a lot of hosting service providers, and you can select one within your budget. However, most domain names range between $8 and $15 a year.

Choosing a Website

A website design dictates how your website design is structured and how your information and products are presented to your clients. Therefore, you should concentrate on buying a professional website template/theme. Compared to Amazon, where they only maintain your details, the Shopify platform allows you to customize your shop completely., There is little room for customizing your store on Amazon. This can be very pleasant if done properly!

There are many free Shopify e-commerce themes on the Internet, and as simple as this may be, t is highly recommended to spend an extra coin on purchasing a professionally designed theme. This is the case because the more distinct your store is and does not feel like any other online shop, the higher your brand recognition and sales grow.

It is highly recommended that you set aside some cash to employ a new designer to create and build your store from scratch if you do not have the skills to do so. As we saw earlier in chapter one, a true entrepreneur knows when he needs professional help to make the business a success. This allows you to make a complex and perhaps complex store your accurate taste. If you are undecided, don't get too stuck at the end of the day in the theme. It is more essential to do this than to just waste time waiting.

Choosing Niche Products

You can end up being absorbed by the many options accessible as a first-time beginner to shop dropshipping, and this can result in confusion. Fortunately, Shopify has supplied a free spy tool to simplify the procurement method for niche products. The instrument provides you with stunning and accurate data about particular shops, their income, and profit, the marketing strategies employed by the shop and even the subjects that they have bought. This software is called Shopify Exchange.

It is usually only used for the sale, conversion, and purchase of Shopify stores, and many prefer it because of the useful and accurate data it provides. You will know exactly what I mean by the incredible amount of data that the platform provides when you step on the internet to explain your niche and product choices.

Get to understand and use the platform as a spy tool. Seek your data and therefore recommend your decision, filter on-sale stores. It is the perfect tool for printing normal dropshipping stores on demand! Also, make sure to check back every day while stores are updated every hour and new stores open and sell old stores.

Finding Products

Aliexpress products can normally be found on the website of those who are new to Shopify. It's a Chinese marketplace, for those of you who don't understand Aliexpress, where you can get something even a canoe! This website relieves you from the troubles of being concerned with hustles and head problems of getting your inventory upfront or even shipping, AliExpress makes it very easy to locate products you may be interested in adding to your shop for selling. In other words, many Shopify beginners generally take it as the first choice.

But again, I'll let you know something that somewhere along the way you will ultimately know–AliExpress is not the only dropshipping source that vendors have to depend on.

You must know that dropshipping is a company model, so as soon as you decide to sign up, dropshipping is not just "dropshipping AliExpress," you can literally dropship from any supplier.

So many people don't know what the truth here is the game. Their benefits over AliExpress can be drawn literally from eBay, Amazon, and DHGate and they cut down shipping times by almost half. The only thing AliExpress has in addition to the options is that the price is usually the cheapest and the most affordable products available.

The following advantages can be derived from dropshipping from other sources apart from Aliexpress:

➢ You appreciate a greater variety of goods and generally have a better quality
➢ You benefit from a reduction in the delivery period.
➢ You store from trustworthy suppliers.

Fulfillment automation

It is extremely advisable for you to use a free tool known as the Oberlo application to use AliExpress as your dropshipping partner. This app simplifies the import method and the purchasing method for customers. It's the best dropping partner for beginners and it is a must-have, especially when freely available. Go on and download the App once Shopify is turned on and the Chrome plugin for Google can also be accessed by pressing the button on AliExpress products.

It's a little more complicated if you talk of dropshipping for eBay, Amazon, or DHGate. At the time of writing, there is no software component for these schemes that encourages compliance and import of products. The only viable method of managing these orders is to use a virtual assistant to manually fulfill the commands when you start to see a big amount of orders in the above mentioned three schemes.

Finding the Right Supplier

The dropshipping model of doing business is quite different from other models of doing business, I both the offline and traditional e-commerce businesses. In a dropshipping business, you are not required to come up with a supply chain and maintain it. It is important for you however to nurture your suppliers. This is because it is their duty to set product prices, shipping dates, terms of payment, and also determining whether or not an item is available for sale.

It is therefore essential for you to have a good business relationship with your suppliers. To ensure this, you can note down the following pointers:

➢ Timely payment is important so as to ensure you are a valued customer.

- ➢ Put in place achievable goals in terms of your expected sales during a specific period of time.
- ➢ Always have in mind that you are not the only customer they are catering to.
- ➢ Make a point of learning everything that is required of you whenever you are making an order.
- ➢ Instead of throwing around blame whenever anything goes wrong, work with the supplier's representative to make sure that the situation is taken care of in a timely and professional manner.
- ➢ It is very advantageous to make friends with the supplier's representative. Business is always conducted much more smoothly whenever you are dealing with a friendly person.
- ➢ Make sure that you make the representative aware of your specific needs for better service. Such needs may include updated product photos, notifications regarding stock outages, product changes, price updates, and discontinued products.

How to Spot an Illegitimate Shopify Dropshipping Supplier/Wholesaler

After searching for a niche market, you will need to do some research on the suppliers that you will be dealing with. This is because the efficiency and professionalism of your supplier are directly related to the success of your business. The more professional and efficient a supplier is, the happier your customers will be and the more business you are bound to get.

The unfortunate this, however, is that the best wholesalers out here are not that aggressive in marketing themselves and therefore are harder to fund. The simple implication of this is that fake suppliers will be the ones who will appear most in your search results. You will, therefore, need to be equipped with the necessary skills to ensure that you can be able to identify these fake or illegitimate suppliers. The following pointers will help you identify these traders and make it easier to avoid them.

1. Ongoing Fees

If you find a supplier that charges a recurring fee to allow you to order from them then chances are that they are fake suppliers. Legitimate or real wholesalers will never ask you for a recurring, membership or any other fee in order for you to order from them. You need to make sure that you are conducting your search in the wholesaler's directory where they are categorized according to the market or product type. More so, wholesalers in this list are usually vetted and verified to be legitimate.

2. Selling to the Public

In order for you to sell at actual wholesale prices, you need to have for a wholesaler account. For your wholesaler account to be approved, your physical business needs to be vetted and verified to make sure it is legitimate, and it is a real business. There are high chances that 'wholesalers' who are offering their products to the general public at wholesale prices are fake. They are just retailers who are selling at inflated wholesale prices.

3. Dropshipping Fees

In this industry, packaging and shipping of individual or small orders are more expensive than the cost incurred when processing bulk orders. Legitimate dropshippers will always charge a standard dropshipping fee that ranges from $2 to $5.

4. Minimum Order Size

Some wholesalers have a policy on the minimum order size of the first order that you place with them. The minimum order size is the lowest amount that your order should be for the supplier to process the order. This is usually done so as to filter out real shoppers form those who are just window shopping. For dropshippers, this may result in a world of problems for dropshippers. For example, if you have a supplier that requires your first order to have a value of $200 but your first order is only worth $50, it would be pointless to spend the $200 because you will make a loss and this beats the purpose of running the business. The best way to safeguard your business from this is by negotiating with your supplier to let you prepay the $200 and have it as store credits. This means that you can utilize this $200 to pay for a number of orders and profitably run your business.

Finding a Dropshipping Supplier on Shopify

Now the difficult portion is finished. With your favorite selection of products, you have developed, personalized and stored your online shop, so the simple portion goes, making some good money now.

Best Shopify Starter Apps

Besides making sales online incredibly easy, Shopify also provides online stores with free and premium tools that they can use to increase their chances of succeeding in their eCommerce business venture when coupled with the business model of dropshipping.

If you want to boost your revenue from the beginning, the Shopify App Store is a tool to use entirely.

The library of the applications that are accessible is somewhat overwhelming and, to be honest, certain apps are not great. In the app store at Shopify with over 2000 apps–and expanding! It can be a mission to find the gems and to find the right gems for your business.

Whether you want to add customer feedback, improve email marketing, generate personal proof to increase income or increase customer service surveillance, the following is a list of the top six apps that have been suggested by individuals when you first start your store. Best of all, they're all completely secure!

They have premium properties, of course, and again it is highly advisable to use the paid versions if you scaling your store and find out the apps that are beneficial, because most of the previous apps are valuable.

Oberlo
Oberlo is the greatest tool to use when you buy your AliExpress products and sell them in your shop. It's basically an app that you can use to achieve the following:

1. Quite simply import AliExpress goods straight into your shop.
2. Complete many orders automatically with a few clicks, no matter how large they are.

This is basically an easy way to scale up your business when it is at this particular point. You can use Oberlo free of charge until you have more than 500 products in your store. When the number of products in your store exceeds the threshold of 500 products, you will have to upgrade your subscription package and at this point, it will simply be pocket change to you.

Aftership

Aftership is different from the rest of the shipping apps. In particular, their app enables you to track all your messages and guidelines in one place–helpful for THAT now. They partner with almost all conceivable couriers and are able to sort shipments according to dates, status, shipments, and locations. This gives your valuable customers a way to check that your shipments are sent on time.

It is highly simple to implement this app in your store, where customers simply enter the tracking numbers rather than calling on you or your customer support team. Simply create your logo and link it to your store via a personalized landing page. You may also use AfterShip with a premium account to notify customers of shipments, delivery, and other exceptions when their orders are in delivery. AfterShip's app can offer your customers superior services and be a good complement to your business management.

Loox

In other words, Loox is an imaging tool that enables you to access AliExpress accounts with a single click! This is a must-get app for new stores because it gives credibility and much-needed social evidence to drive income otherwise in a baron store. Loox also facilitates the upload of images by your customers from themselves receiving, transporting or using your products, using feedback from customers and user content.

These mobile images are displayed and arranged in visually appealing galleries or in a dedicated review section underneath the item page. A broad variety of embedded features are also available, such as comprehensive customization (planning, color, size, place, branding). You can also moderate reviews, incorporate Google's review for SEO, take a quick look into collections and customer pages, selling options, localizing opportunities, and more.

Happy Email

The relationship between your customers is so important, and this app automates this process saving you so much time. Happy Email automatically allows you to send an email of thanks to your customers 30 minutes after making their first purchase or to register for the first time in your store.

The email will be released based on your information and client conduct. Fortunately, you won't have to care about anything other than the one-click setup and personalized messages.

Happy Email Shop app is the easiest way to thank your customers. You don't even have to write your own materials, the app automatically sends emails.

MailChimp

I have always championed how significant email addresses are to be gathered and you have to start as soon as the Shop is set up live! Once you have the email addresses, you will want to start some operations. You can choose from many internet service providers to find the one that best suits your business needs.

You want to work with a provider that offers not only a number of useful features but also can scale with your firm. What does the system do? MailChimp is one of the most popular email management techniques available and it is not without reason. It is a great tool to design and organize campaigns, send automated posts and much more.

Best Currency Converter

It is the highest currency converter, as its name indicates. It does a nice job to make sure your clients are satisfied with local currency. The risk of shopping carts being abandoned and client frustration when attempting to change the currency significantly decreases.

Shop Optimization

You need to optimize it now, as you have accomplished nearly all you need to create your site a real online store. Optimization of your website is essential because it is one of the greatest approaches for beginners to guarantee conversion and higher revenues. In addition to selecting goods and advertising policies, it is very critical to ensure that your shop's frontline is at its finest and best accomplished before you begin riding internet traffic.

The storefront is the most significant commercial instrument you have for an online shop. It determines how your company is perceived at first sight by your clients. Usually, there is no second opportunity for a first impression, so you should not take the opportunity to do that.

Tips for Store Optimization

I won't tell you, however, of the importance of optimizing your store and not showing you how. Tips for optimizing your website So, I thought I would share some tips (if you haven't already, of course) on stuff to alter in your store to improve immediately your percentage of conversion.

These changes generally focus on retaining trust and loyalty but have a relatively big impact. When I started and saw an increase of approximately 5 additional profits per day, I personally made the following changes. Especially if you have a greater average selling price.

Removing Getting Rid of the Shipping and Taxes section a Checkout

➤ Go to your Shopify admin panel and navigate to the *Language* Section
➤ Go to the *Manage Checkout Language* option.
➤ Click on the *Cart* tab at the top of the page
➤ Scroll down and find the sentence, either *deleting or editing it.*

Psychologically, after adding the item to the cart, clients do not like seeing a prospective premium on top of the price of the item. Personally, I like managing free delivery campaigns, so I was successful in altering the line to "FREE Shipping Included," which clearly provides them additional motivation to continue to the next move, checkout and eventually transform.

Removing Order Notes

➢ Navigate to the *Theme Settings* section of your Shopify Admin Panel.

➢ Click on *Settings*

➢ Click on *Cart* on the left-hand side of the panel

➢ Uncheck *Order Notes*

➢ This process may vary depending on the theme you have chosen for your shop.

Unless you're in the business of selling products that require clients to send a note during, I would suggest that you remove this section altogether as it is an unnecessary object that can prevent the client from converting to a sale. The faster the streamlined and easier method of checkout.

Remove 'Powered by Shopify'

➢ Navigate to the *Online Store* section of your Shopify Admin Panel.

- ➢ Click on *Themes*
- ➢ Click on *Actions > Edit Code*
- ➢ In the sections folder, open the *Footer Liquid File*
- ➢ On your keyboard, click *CTRL + F* and search for the following piece of code: *{{ powered_by_link }}*.
- ➢ Delete that tag

This is simple but it ensures that the website remains independent and professional looking. This link is only beneficial to Shopify but is useless to your business; it is actually disadvantageous to you.

Equip your Product Pages with Trust Badges

- ➢ Navigate to the *Online Store* section of your Shopify Admin Panel.
- ➢ Click on *Themes*
- ➢ Click on *Actions > Edit Code*
- ➢ In the sections folder, open the *Product Template Liquid File*
- ➢ On your keyboard, click *CTRL + F* and search for *addtocart.*
- ➢ Add the piece of code that contains your business' trust seal that is hosted on Cloudfront or CDN.

You should be careful not to flood your site with trust badges because it makes your website look untidy and more suspicious than a site without these badges at all.

Customize your Add to Cart Button

➤ Navigate to the *Online Store* section of your Shopify Admin Panel.

➤ Click on *Themes*

➤ Click on *Actions > Edit Code*

➤ In the sections folder, open the *theme.scss.liquid File*

➤ On your keyboard, click *CTRL + F* and search for *Link and Button Styles.* it is important for you to note that some themes have a different for this section so you have to be keen on this.

➤ At the end of this section and just before the following section, add the following piece of code:

```
#AddToCart { width: 380px; }
```

Even when trust tags are attached to the product section, this is often missed. Changing the size of the ATC button is crucial in order to stay a consumer website focal point as we clearly want as many clients to tap on it. Also worth adding to the header and checkout header trust badges by manually changing your Photoshop logo and adding trust tags.

Pros and Cons of Dropshipping using Shopify

Pros of Dropshipping using Shopify

Minimal Startup Capital

The Shopify dropshipping platform provides the smallest subscription fees compared to other dropshipping platforms. As a beginner, you get full package access for 14 days in a package of your choice. During this time, you can test all the tools and you can pay for your monthly subscriptions from as low as $29 if you decide that Shopify is the proper place for your business. You are free to close down your store if you decide to take another route.

Minimal overhead variable costs

The variable operating costs incurred when running a Shopify dropshipping company are very small since you do not need to have high operating costs. In addition to marketing and monthly subscribers, you do not incur many variable operating costs and hence more profitability at Shopify.

Online Store Customization

Unlike other e-retail systems, Shopify allows company owners to customize their store online to their individual requirements. The company logo and even style your store framework as you want can be uploaded.

Convenient Product Sourcing

Through its many associations with other professionals in the industry, Shopify makes it simple for you to acquire goods and incorporate them into your shop. Tools are accessible in your administrative board to support you in the growth of your company by getting the finest and most qualified vendors.

Professional and Simple Platform

The Shopify Platform is professionally designed to keep your company stress-free. Professional and easy to use Platform The platform is easy to operate and so you don't spend much time attempting to know about the system.

Quick Startup

Time to get started The Shopify team understands you have to start your company as soon as possible. They have therefore developed their platform in order to keep your company operational, taking minimal time. You can get your company internet prepared to begin trading in about 30 minutes.

Location Flexibility

Shopify is a worldwide supplier and associates business in all countries. This allows you the freedom to distribute your products worldwide. You don't simply sell and deliver in your town or nation.

Shopify makes sure that they are doing their best to ensure that the manufacturers and suppliers of their platform are legit and supply products up to standard in order to achieve a high level of reliance with sellers using the Shopify Dropship platform. You are confident that your clients will obtain the excellent value products they buy with alliances with other e-retail giant companies including Amazon, Alibaba, and eBay.

Easy operation

The management of your company is simple under the Shopify dropshipping platform. You only market the company and handles customer service problems once you bring the products you want to sell into your shop. The storage, storage and shipping issues will not matter to you since this will be handled without your involvement by providers and mail associates.

Cons of Shopify Dropshipping

Low-Profit Margins

This is the biggest disadvantage for shoplifting, especially when you are working in a highly competitive niche. Because shopping is so easy and the costs are small, more and more people establish stores and shopping at the lowest possible prices to try to get the money. These people invest little in starting up their business to enable them to create the lowest earnings.

In many circumstances, these dealers are probable to have very unprofessional websites and non-existent client service, but this does not stop future customers from sharing ratings –and will be the lowest as most of the time. Your profit margins are very small due to the large competition.

Inventory problems

When you run an enterprise where you hold your own stock, it is comparatively easy to track which item is in stock, low or out of stock. But you depend on other suppliers when you choose to use Shopify dropshipping, and these suppliers not only provide their customers but also serve other retailers ' production requirements. Therefore, every day their inventory quantities change. You can use systems to sync your store inventory with your suppliers ' store, but that won't work well all the time and some suppliers won't encourage the necessary technologies. This may be extremely annoying for your customers if they think that they are prepared to purchase an item just to see that it's out of stock and have to wait longer for an item they've already paid for or wait until a refund is processed before they are able to purchase from another retailer.

Shipping Problems

Most shippers work with various separate suppliers, and many shippers supply the products that you deliver. This system can cause issues with delivery costs. Let us assume, for example, that three different products have been ordered by a customer. All this comes from different suppliers, which means that you pay three sets of shipping costs, one for each item. It's not very intelligent to transfer these costs to your customers since they assume you charge for the shipping and it's not easy to automate the cost calculations, even if you choose to do this. The finest way of doing it is with average shipping expenses between the suppliers, some of which you spend some money on, and others.

This may also trigger customers to get angry when they order three products from one store and send them to all three products individually. The monitoring of your orders and with three separate monitoring numbers makes it more difficult for customers to feel controlled. The improved confusion which can arise if a customer attempts to find support with one single product but has combined order numbers or surveillance numbers is also a feasible issue.

Disputes with Suppliers

Another problem of operating a Shopify dropshipping business to use sellers to dispute your customer issues is that things can go wrong. There are times when you and your retailers don't follow the same line, from technical issues to misunderstandings.

How many times have to take the blame even for issues that are clearly not your fault. Even the top providers of dropshipping sometimes make mistakes and it is up to you to take charge of the mistakes and apologize. If you use poor quality suppliers, you will face more challenges than you can afford with issues such as missing goods from shipments, defective goods, and poor quality packaging— they may not be your fault but your reputation and that of the business will suffer.

Another thing to remember while running a business with suppliers of dropshipping is that most internet distributors work with more than one product client. This can rapidly become complicated since there is no standard for data dimensions. This means that things can be different from order handling, account setup and billing from one supplier to the next. This can contribute to complex and costly contacts with providers when the information is mixed between providers. This should be remembered when you are vetting your vendors.

Chapter 3: Amazon

Sellers nowadays have a ton of choices to choose from, because so many blogs on the internet have appeared. People can buy their things on so many sites, selling their old things quickly and easily. If that is what you want, you can also begin a serious company. Most of these e-commerce sites worry nothing about this. It can, therefore, be hard to choose between common types of e-commerce platforms.

Private Labeling

Private branding is currently very common, so you likely must have heard of it. Most internet retailers now use private labeling for their goods. This provides the goods with a distinctive image, showcasing the brand of the seller. Private branding also enables to stronger market and to build your brand's credibility. But how does it all happen?

First, to distribute them under your brand name, you purchase the products from your provider. Actually, you're not making them, which is the standard way of conducting business. You develop a private brand and then placed all the products you purchased under that brand to resell. To do this, the custom names on the products and their bundles have to be edited and (if any) the prior product names deleted. This guarantees that the client does not combine the item with the manufacturer's brand. This approach is currently highly common and is used by most internet vendors. You can find companies that can assist you to create a brand identity for yourself. You will be encouraged to expand, promote and place your brand in the industry so that you can create the finest of it.

The Importance of Private Labeling

Easier to manage: it is easy to trade than to produce, which is fairly evident. In contrast, it is much less difficult so discard any misunderstandings you may have about personal branding. Some people think it's the only way to have private-label goods is to produce your own products, and not by buying them. Nobody knows about who produced an item of excellent value that you are offered at a fair price. It's a smart choice to avoid enormous expenses and distribute under a personal tag.

Modification: You can modify products in accordance with your requirements and desires with personal branding privileges. You can therefore uniquely manufacture your products without developing innovative brand thoughts. Take goods already on the industry and modify them a little bit to offer them a character. Private labeling differs from reselling because you can not modify reselling privileges that do not apply to personal labeling privileges. Come and introduce fresh thoughts into your product design. Do what you want, it's your item!

Customer Satisfaction: Private branding facilitates your company's voyage by withdrawing measures. First of all, you do not need to waste money on the conceptualization of products, which is by the manner quite hard when doing personal packaging. Even if you have a nice brand idea, someone will probably do it faster than you and you must begin again. In virtually every niche there are many giants, so trying to defeat them at their own match is useless. Purchase the products instead and offer them your personal brand. You can thus focus on other significant items, such as fulfillment for the client. You will pay your clients the utmost consideration because there are no things to care about such as personal administration, product planning, effectiveness monitoring, and other major duties.

Bandwagon rides: It's always dangerous when you bring a fresh item on the shelf. In essence, new concepts appear to be such. You're going to be a great flop or a great hit most of the time and you can't be sure. If the item succeeds, a large percentage of mistake leaves it costly and hard for the producer. For everybody, it's not the way. However, it is much easier to use private labeling. Do not care about wasting cash, as you can choose an already famous item and buy it for the advantage of its reputation under your own personal label brand. With minimal attempt and without spending much cash on advertising, you will be given a client foundation.

How to Choose the Best Private Label Products for Amazon

One of Amazon's most common sales methods is personal labeling, but most individuals have an issue in determining which products to buy, which are the best ones to construct a brand of their own. Some individuals choose the complex path, select products that need a bunch of change and price a fortune to create and some choose the easy path.

The first issue I have to answer is why you choose personal branding. Most individuals use Amazon to build their brand are those who want to discover proper products on eBay that Amazon can make a profit or vice versa. Reselling is not a nice match–you may get a bit more money, but it never will be steady earnings and a bunch of work. Private tag goods offer you the greatest opportunity for continuous and comparatively active revenue while maintaining minimum and overhead work and time. The true advantages of constructing a brand around private label products are seen by many without having to look continuously for fresh ones in order to maintain the cash going. There is, however, one enormous obstacle to real achievement, an unwanted complication.

It's simple to see the advantages of brand construction, but as the item you choose is more complicated, more research must be done, and that should contribute to a far greater likelihood of income generation. All right, that might be true; after all, the iPhone is much more precious than the plastic food packaging, but it doesn't imply that constructing an iPhone will get individuals. The better you succeed, the more cash you create, the more easy things will emerge. With crush, your brand's finest private label products are easy, and if you comply with these regulations, they will work. Just bring your cash to a specific product before you ask yourselves these issues:

a) Is it perennial? Will your client continue to return to it, over and over again? Think of stuff like shampoos or conditioners–things individuals are going to purchase over and over.

b) Are the individuals searching for your item? Imagine just threw a few thousand bucks on an item, labeled it and then discovered that no-one was searching for it. The sort of your item is not only your real brand. What are you going to think like? Awesome? Dumb? There's an easy way to figure out what individuals on Amazon are looking for before you spend your lives, and that's to check the Amazon keyword. You can do this by entering a search bar with particular keywords in Amazon and seeing the outcomes, you can use one of the numerous automated registration instruments. Some of these instruments inform you what has been looked for in particular lists, and others recognize differences in the industry in which you can believe.

c) Having loads of rivalry in your item? You may have a difficult time getting your foot at the gate if you choose an item that is very prevalent in Amazon.

But there are a number of products that do not compete and these are those you should read at. Although the item has competition, consider if the competition can not end up with something like multiples.

d) How simple and inexpensive is the item? You do not have to buy high-cost products that price a fortune and require a bunch of change. Selling 15 plastic container packaging devices every day at $20 would be safer than selling a device once in a while as an exceptionally low-profit margin.

e) Does the item have demonstrated marketing information? One move many individuals overlook is to test your Amazon account with retail products before you choose to put a total purchase. This is a significant move to show if your item is to be sold by a supplier before you begin your costly sourcing process.

Actually, nothing is too science or hard. Private labels are simply the best products to offer. Items that are going to hold the time test, products that individuals repeatedly return to.

5 More private label rules Selling on Amazon

In the meantime, you ought to understand how to sell Amazon on private labels. But there are still some people who believe that it will be an easy task and that they can create cash immediately. The following are the five most important rules for sellers of Amazon's personal labels.

You need capital

This is the most important rule–you can not create cash from buying a private tag unless you are equipped first. Without having a lot of capital, to begin with, you can not purchase your inventory, create your brand, and construct your packaging. The creation of the private label of your own is NOT like the finding of a re-invented Amazon product. You need the cash to purchase your item on a regular basis, to compensate for changes you could wish, which is not free of charge. Initially, your suppliers won't give you the best deal on a product you choose and they won't construct prototypes unless you buy a large quantity-that implies a bunch of cash. If you have it or are unwilling to settle, go and discover another way, because you're losing money.

There are no Quick Wins

There is a huge difference between those who resell Amazon and those who create their own products and brands. You are not going to get any quick victories. The latter build an asset that will bring the money into the foreseeable future, while a reseller will simply make immediate money and must go to sell another product afterward. These two character kinds have a universe of distinction. Everybody intends to create cash but the individual building an asset understands that although the goods only get an additional $100 a month, they are considerably higher and last much longer than the individual flipping a costly item. Why is that? Why?

Assets are always a stronger choice than simply getting the expertise to shuffle a single item. Assets have more sustainable value and are long-lasting. It is much easier for you to have ten stocks worth $5,000 each month, then every month, resell goods you spin once, and they're disappeared.

Know your Customers and Minimise Risks

One of the most lucrative methods to succeed in a personal brand item is to understand precisely who your clients are and to comprehend them. And Amazon Sponsored Ads are the best way to know your clients. The dumbest thing to do is select an item and speak to your provider, purchase a whole stack and put it on Amazon and expect a lot of cash to be made. It can operate, but it is quite uncommon. When producing your personal tag item, you need to maintain your hazards small. Test your item with Amazon Sponsored Ads so that individuals really want it and plug into their wallets. You have to change your attitude, but you have to learn how to take advantage of these sponsored ads before paying for something you can't change.

You are not an Amazon Reseller

So stop feeling like a lot of individuals are troubled, feeling like an Amazon reseller and not like a personal brand vendor. You are not an Amazon reseller. You have to invest time in creating your product and resources to be effective and operate a true company. A reseller needs to begin again every week or month to seek out this next large item and process its shipment and everything that comes along with it. The goods that they construct are trying to produce cash with very little input from you. A private label vendor that has accomplished its homework can construct something much larger than it is, something that is long-lasting.

Don't Forget to Build on the Success of Your Work

Don't forget to develop on and most significantly, construct on the achievement of your work. The cash you gain from your item requires to be created and supported. It's so appealing to give up and invest your income, but the more you plugin, the more you get out. like anything. You have to remember that it is not simple to produce, and a very unusual individual will come to your house for the first time, to be able to successfully sell private label products. Do not fear, do your assignments before you purchase them and begin tiny and experiment with your goods. Build your company as you do it and, if you do it correctly, you will ultimately have a solid asset with little feedback.

These are excellent enough grounds to persuade you. You should certainly regard personal branding as an internet distributor as this will bring your company much quicker to the next stage.

Importance of Samples

This is a significant component to bear in mind. We'll inform you to have a sample, but you have to ask why this is so essential. You understand, after all, what your item feels like; you understand how it operates, so why are you looking for a sample?

First, you can seek to purchase an item that requires a little change to render it really unique. You have to see what this sample sounds like, how it operates, whether it operates and whether it is what you want. At least three samples of your item should be ordered if possible, particularly when you make adjustments. Ask for a sample of each color if you are offered it in various colors. In order to create sure the products are correct, you want to see how the samples are placed into your selection of packages. You would not know whether it was a single item or the manner in which it was normally packaged to order only one sample, and was only thrown in the box without any kind of padding. This issue will be answered by ordering a number of samples.

Costings

The price will clearly increase, and so will the costs of the samples when you customize your item. You've ordered three and paid for shipping The samples would cost you $300, and for arguments you would be charged $150 (these were big items, obviously smaller, one cost less); You have ordered a $100 sample (these are figures plucked out of the air, don't hurry, do not!). There's $450 for your three samples to generate and deliver. Now, it may look like a bunch of cash for samples, but its essential here.

Initially, you can see the product quality. You could figure out you were possibly vending a bit of ill-made garbage only by going ahead and buying thousands of devices without checking them out. You are able to see what the samples are as before by paying the cash. Powerful products will only gain you a lot of refund applications and a poor record. Second, you can see every item variety and see which items can be finest worked and which items could be dropped. Third, you can check the item for yourself and you can invest all the cash. You will at least understand that the item is working and value.

How to use the Samples

When you take those samples, you first check the quality of the samples, but there are a couple of other tasks you can do to get out your money. The finest methods to use your samples are:

1. Take High-Quality Product Photos

If your supplier sends you a picture of your product, they do not have the best quality and certainly do not represent very well what you are selling. People like to see nice, transparent photos of an item they want, and images of bad performance are a major turnaround. Many clients use the images to determine whether the product is to be purchased or not so that you need the best images you can. With the sample, every variation, and every color can be photographed, and the product can also be taken from various angles. Take your pictures with a good camera or smartphone and get the utmost you can without the need for a qualified photographer. You can give one example back and still have a pair remaining if you discover that you have to use professionals.

2. Right Packaging

Make sure your vendors will give you photos of the product, but two factors are what you see in the photo and what the product truly feels like. In certain cases, you may not even be aware of the package's appearance. The stuff that packages the item in the delivery container is the packaging I am speaking about here.

Let's claim you've requested an iPad box. In the packaging inside the cabinet, the order will arrive. If you want, a cabinet within a cabinet. In order to assist construct your own brand awareness, you must know first-hand that you can add your own brand and fashion logo to the packaged, which does not have to be simple. Use your samples to determine what ad you want in the packaging and tell the provider that you want to make any change. You're first of all going to see your packaging: if it's not correct, you won't trust much of the item itself. You can also use it to publicize your own page and create additional advertising and revenues.

3. Get Feedback

This is one of the greatest stuff you can do with your samples. Use them to get feedback. Show your family and friends to other individuals and request for feedback from them. As a proprietor of an item, you have a certain inclination and it is nice to receive the views of other people, if you like, a cool number of gaze. Take a few days to use the test, then apply for advice–meaningful, not harmful.

Something may be wrong, something small you couldn't see, but a "stranger." Get as much feedback as you can before you go with your item online. Check that the item does precisely what you are supposed to do, while you are here. All this is to confirm not only your item but also your choice.

4. Use Them in Your Marketing Strategy

Use your advertising approach is essential to your company achievement and that's exactly what personal brand goods are–a company. Please take and use these photos on your social network sites anywhere you believe to advertise, not only on your account but also in your blog. You might even produce a brief clip of the item shown and upload it. Use or upload it to YouTube on your personal websites. Videos are great methods to attract potential clients because they can indeed see how the item operates and because it definitely operates for the desired intent.

5. Test the durability of your item

Push your item to the extent possible, ensure it is stable and does not crack first. Put the samples in the dishwasher on several occasions if you are advertising your item safely for the dishwasher. Make secure that it has some hard water trials if you claim it is waterproof. Test it and ensure that the item is secure to dry and then add a dryer. By pressing it to its complete threshold, you are almost trying to crack your item. You have to make sure the product works as you say–if you don't, a series of poor feedback and poor notoriety will result in you.

6. Check the Specifications

Check and check the sample for the item requirements provided to you by the provider. Care should be taken to determine if the specification states it is 5 inches high by 10 inches broad and averages 5 libraries. Measure and measure, ensure the correct weight and length. To verify that your item is what you and the provider say it is, check all the requirements. It must suit your advertisement; it is so easy.

7. Testing, testing, and testing

Your sample must be checked and tested, if needed, for demolition. You must understand how lengthy it's short-lasting, how far it can be driven and what it can do. Make sure you spend a thousand bucks in this item; an item that you understand is of the value you think that it is. You take a huge danger when you place your very first command, so create sure that you sell something first.

Opening a Seller Account

Amazon provides you with a great chance to make money online. You can get additional revenue or even leave your work and establish a full-time Amazon company if you like. It provides you much liberty and more than what you bring in.

Let us look at some advantages of trading on Amazon:

> ➢ Flexible job timetable and liberty of play.
> ➢ Financial security.
> ➢ Good yields on your investments.
> ➢ Further open space for your favorite activities.

➤ Further experience in future major initiatives.

➤ It is very simple to know to do, and the greatest part about that is.

➤ You monitor your company's profitability. You define how effective you are in the implementation of these policies.

You will also gradually understand the ins and outs of your business, and this will increase your revenue further. But all this is coming subsequently. We need to begin with a few child measures right now.

The first move you take to start your company is to set up an Amazon Seller account. The method is quite simple. You don't have to follow anything else, Amazon gives useful advice to get through you readily.

1) Open the following URL in your internet browser https://services.amazon.com/. It will make the process easier for you here!

2) If you press the "Start Selling" button.

3) You'll be taken to another section where you will find a login form, but since at this point you want to open an account, you will click on the "Create an Amazon Account" button in order to start the registration process.

4) Once you submit the registration form, you will receive a one time password (OTP) in your email address, that you will need to enter so as to verify your email address and continue with the registration process.

5) Once you successfully do this, you will be prompted to enter your business location and the type of business you are running. If your country is not listed, then you do not qualify to operate an Amazon business.

6) Once done with the registration process, you will need to choose whether you will sell as a "person" or as a "business." Consider the distinctions between the two.

   a.   A customer can purchase only up to 40 products per month. A vendor can buy any amount of products in a month, on the other side. No constraints are in place.

   b.   A fee of 99 dollars for every product that he offers is paid to an individual vendor. In this situation, there is no monthly charge. In contrast, a vendor paid a monthly charge of $39.99. Some extra costs, such as referral charges and variable closure charges, may sometimes be payable in both ways.

c. Professional vendors can offer products for all Amazon classifications. This cannot be done by individual vendors. In a restricted amount of classifications, they can be sold. It is, therefore, recommendable for you to go with your company strategy.

7) You will need to read and register a seller's contract once you select a scheme.

8) Before you continue, print out this Agreement. In the future, you will be helped iron every problem. Upon reading it, accept the terms and conditions and continue on.

9) You will have to complete certain significant data in the next section, such as your credit card details, payment number, vendor names, and company email.

10) You must check your identification after that. You will receive a PIN by SMS or a call to an amount you provide. This is a normal method followed by many locations.

11) In order to continue, a professional vendor must also provide Amazon with the required income data.

12) The enrollment process will be concluded when you have given your tax data and you will be transferred to the Seller Central account's web site.

All operations on your behalf can be managed from here.

Configuring your seller profile

You will need to finish your public profile once you have enabled your account. This is what potential clients will view as a Facebook or Twitter variant of Amazon. Your clients will learn who you are, about your company and the shipping services that you deliver. You will see your return policy; other clients can see feedback and more. The most important parts of your website are the following.

About Seller

This chapter will present you and your company to your clients. You have to inform individuals precisely who you are, how your company began, how it was inspired. Tell your clients about the ideology of your company, what you want to accomplish and deliver and inform them anything that is important. You try to establish a link with your clients and must be as transparent as feasible. This helps to create confidence and will allow your clients to choose your competitors.

Your Logo

Your clients will see your logo on your shop front and on your At a glance list at various locations including an offer listing website. Keep your logo to 120x 30 centimeters and do not include your website's URLs or quotes.

Return and Refund Policy

Give your clients complete directions about how to transfer refund or substitution products. 3-Your transfer and refund policies. Please inform them about the email they need to submit payments and how soon a refund is to bring or submit a substitute item. When you create your regulations, take into account that Amazon requires all vendors to allow clients to exchange their products for a duration of at least 30 days after purchase.

With this data in advance, you can begin booking your product and make cash from your Amazon Seller Central account!

Choosing a great product

This is probably the main move in the entire method. If you don't select a murderer item, all will be for nothing. Why does it matter so much? Just because the only manner you can perform in your company is to select a good-selling item. It must be marketable if an item is to be marketed more. You can't do your company job without an excellent item. So what's "good" for a commodity? Let's glance at some key variables.

Good volume sales

This is a basic principle in selecting an excellent item. You want this item to be sold so you have to ensure it is well sold on the industry. You won't profit from it if you select a niche product that buys only a few pieces each month. The industry is too competitive, so you have to choose an item which is large. But it is also essential that you ensure that this item is not already sold by large competitors in the industry. These vendors dominate the companies they sell and take up the largest proportion of the industry by buying on small returns. Because small sellers can't benefit from big markets.

Attractive Pricing

You must understand how essential it is to bring your item at the correct cost if you are accurate with a cognitive idea called impulsive purchasing. You must select an item that fits in the correct cost range for this purpose. They should be big enough to make it look unusable but inexpensive enough to make individuals experience the desire to purchase it as quickly as they see the cost. We call this "impulsive purchase." When the client believes that the cost is not too large, she does not imagine comparing comparable goods to give you a sustainable benefit.

You can't choose a product that is cheap because you don't benefit from it since you have to charge certain charges to Amazon. Between $20 and $100 is the highest value. Choose an item below $50 if you want to improve it further.

Niche Product

Extremely non-niche goods are not going to sell, at least not for your company. So if you thought to go with soap dishes or accessories, give the concept. Your products have to be somewhat distinctive so that they can represent a specific niche. Generic product markets are already extremely saturated, and they're dominated by big players, so you don't want to go there. Instead, you have a particular set of clients to aim, which is not too large or too low, but just the correct amount to return. Sell a product that people don't find easily in supermarkets and centers, which isn't commonplace in every town.

Non-seasonal product

Want to sell all year round? Don't choose a temporary, easy item. You will be astonished by how many individuals do not take this into consideration before selecting the correct item. Choose an item that is not temporary in design if you want to buy all year round. Or if you don't have to use your item, your revenues will fall sharply and it will harm your company. If a temporary item is not available, choose several other products to buy and ensure that some of them are non-seasonal. Throughout the year, you can continue to sell.

Necessary Competition

Not all the contest is poor; you know that before you begin sales. A small seller like you can't afford to invest a lot in your product's publicity, so it's nice to get competitive in your industry. It is good, even beneficial for your company. You will not profit from being the only participant in the industry as you will not be prepared to make your products aware of the marketplace.

Then choose a commodity that is competitively safe. You can reap the advantages of advertising from your rivals. Be careful of over-saturated economies at the same time. As mentioned previously, too much rivalry will destroy your company.

Good providers

Good providers are vital for such a company. You can expect him to produce the correct products on time when you have a nice provider. In turn, this will guarantee that you can deliver on-time commands and create your credibility. A poor provider will, on the other side, be untrustworthy, which could harm your company unless it delivers on time. It is perfect to have a reputable vendor and to have various vendors for your choice of product(s). In this manner, even if one vendor faces some problems, you can create sure your transactions are not impeded.

Mobility

Another significant consideration is the accessibility of your item. You should select an easy-to-ship item because Amazon complies with rigorous norms for shipment and packaging. This allows you to face issues if your item is too brittle, voluminous or readily damaged. To verify the packaging of most products, fall experiments are in location. This determines if they are great for shipping.

Profitability

The most evident is profitability. What does it make for if you can't take advantage of a commodity, correct?

Finally, you're in the company to make profits and you can't do that without a lucrative item. Make sure your item can be sold to you, even after you pay Amazon charges, with reasonable profit margins.

Now that we have looked at some of the key variables in determining which item to distribute, you have to ask how to locate the correct item. Let's offer you the beginning of a hat. The simplest place to begin is to see the bestselling website of the Amazon. This page has been modified every hour and the largest sales products can be found here on the website. Amazon has complicated algorithms that provide very precise and efficient outcomes. Visit the website. Finally, you can discover an item that can be branded and sold readily.

You can also check out other places if this isn't sufficient. The Movers & Shakers chapter and a Hot New Release segment are available on this page, both telling you about goods currently sold well. In the most-wanted segment, Amazon also has request records, so you can look for an understanding. In addition, thoughts can also be found in the Gift Ideas chapter. Make a tiny roster of products and then place each product through the above parameters.

This helps you to select the finest item for sale. If you're still not happy, there are other areas to ˙search for prospective products. Check out eBay, Google Shopping and other famous portals for e-commerce.

> ➢ Check the item requirement by proceeding through the bestsellers ' roster or using the Google Keyword Tool. This is a tiny collection of stuff to do when making a brand decision.
> ➢ Check that the item in existence is not temporary.
> ➢ Check the proper price of the item to promote impulsive purchasing.
> ➢ Check that no major competitors already sell this item on the internet.
> ➢ Make sure that the item is easy to send.
> ➢ Make sure the item is provided with excellent providers.

Finding the Right Suppliers

You need to begin the search for excellent providers for these products once you have one or more products that meet your requirements. This section focuses on how you can quickly and efficiently locate the correct provider for your products. You can go to www.alibaba.com the simplest manner to do this. Alibaba's a trader's blog.

There is a large number of producers and distributors of all kinds of products on this web site. Sellers from around the globe trading in a broad range of products will be present. Traders can email and purchase goods via the internet. As we used to do before the internet, you can still use commercial journals to locate vendors and producers, but Alibaba is certainly the simplest route. It also provides vendors with a number of options.

You can go and discover them on Alibaba after deciding which product(s) you want to offer. For each item, there will be many vendors. Hundreds or even thousands of providers are usually found for an item which causes it very hard to choose one provider. Oh, choosing paradox. However, I'm going to say you something–they're not all-important for you. So, by using the relevant query filter, you can bypass and restrict your query.

Let's get you up to some guidelines quickly. The "Gold Supplier" label is issued to suppliers with a strong record on the internet. Under the provider information, you can test how lengthy a provider holds this position. Then there are vendors that Alibaba or an independent entity verifies. Authorized staff have toured their plant or shop and are mentioned in the "Onsite Check" filter. If a third-party audit firm has checked a provider, it is shown in the screen "Assessed Supplier." This is also accessible for you if you wanted to see the review document. An "escrow" function is accessible to guarantee a secure internet deposit that ensures that the vendor is requested to pay until the products are safely delivered.

Using these filters, your query outcomes will be much reduced. Nevertheless, you will have a bunch to do. From here on you should inspect each seller's price and sales strategy for minimum units. You will discover that in most instances, these figures are negotiable, so get in touch with some vendors before you decide to fix them.

The 6 vendors beginning. Contact each person and let them know your needs. Try to obtain a sample from the providers before you begin negotiations on the prices and the minimum purchase volume. You want prices per device to be reduced without big amounts being purchased at one time.

Talk to them about personal packaging and tell them how you want the products to be marketed. You need to build a brand identity in the industry for yourself. Ask the provider always in advance if they are prepared to mark your products on your personal tag.

Avoid vendors who do not promptly reply to your emails and posts. Shoddy customer service doesn't have to cope with something. Here are some suggestions for helping you:

a.   It requires time to find the correct provider. Before you decide on a supplier, there will be a great deal of success and test, so don't spend your time searching for the right game. Instead, try to get samples from some excellent providers rapidly.

b.   In the future, you are likely to compromise on one provider, but you must begin at the beginning with several providers.

c.   The website of Alibaba is www.aliexpress.com. Here, lower orders can be placed and samples tested.

d.   As your savings, treat your samples. Instead of distributing it on Amazon, test it hard and see how lasting it is. You don't want unsatisfied clients, so that's essential.

e.   It is not essential to place a large first command. Many variables determine the magnitude of your first item: your product, the requirement for the item, the cost per item, and so on. If you need to, begin with the purchasing of a few Aliexpress products.

f. Do not position a big order when you get started, although you have significant assets. You must first perform industry tests to determine the profitability and requirement of the item you are offering. You can begin putting bigger commands once you have measured all this. You can also exchange vendors without failure API you are not satisfied with a single vendor.

g. As your revenue rise and become more coherent, your connection with your supplier(s) will be greater. You will quickly be prepared to receive stronger offers and some may even give further facilities, such as client support and transport. This helps you to automate much of your company.

Shipping Methods

You may not understand that right now, but selecting the correct technique of shipment will have great implications for your company. It is n significant choice to define how your company works. This choice and the accessibility of employees perform a major part in your original purchase. Whatever you begin, you should try to get your products shipped as soon as your company gets on track. Most of your vendors begin personal shipping or Amazon FBA.

Private Shipping

Many individuals begin by converting their garage into a transitional warehouse. You could also start with private shipping if you don't have too much money at the start. Save your products in the garage when you send them to you by your provider, and when you receive an offer send them to your clients. You don't get many commands when you're just beginning, so this method operates well. It helps to give all your commands a private contact. When packaging your product, you can add a personalized note, thank the customer for buying it and share some information about your brand. On this notice, you are able to attach your web address. It puts a positive effect on the client if your item is nice and your packaging effective and enables you to mentally communicate with it.

You need excellent time management for this technique of working because it is of prime significance to shipping products on schedule. Everything is treated individually by you, which can be really motivating or stressful. You have to get to grips with it all. Make sure you change to faster shipping techniques once your company has gone up.

Fulfillment By Amazon (Amazon FBA)

Completion through Amazon This makes completing commands an effective route when you start selling well. It enables you to automate and let Amazon look after a portion of your company. Instead of managing the entire shipping cycle, Amazon pays a tiny price. Ship your products to an Amazon warehouse all you have to do. You may even request your provider to send it to an Amazon warehouse, which reduces your expenses further. That costs you a great deal of cash and time.

Dropshipping

Dropshipping is a common way to ship products at this time. Dropshipping Many internet distributors around the globe use this system. The products are straight forwarded to the clients by the providers. The trader doesn't have a portion, that is to say, you. You must, therefore, be careful not to package and ship the item yourself. If you are a frequent client and a good company to a provider with whom you operate, he will decide to send the goods for you. What else? What else? The provider may even be able to provide you with all customer services that automate your company a lot. Your company evolves to another degree of automation when you establish such a relationship with a provider. You only have to handle the company front end and take care of stuff like sales and product advertising. The provider will provide you with the back end.

Benefits of Amazon

Amazon's benefits are so many stuff that Amazon allows you simple. Here are some reasons to convince Amazon to be the greatest location to begin your e-commerce business –Amazon offers its marketers the most profitable rates. The price is greater than the average price of Amazon, particularly for products sold via FBA (Fulfillment by Amazon) than most other comparable locations, for most products of Amazon. Another excellent thing at Amazon is that clients searching for purchasing choices and convenience are not searching for the smallest rates or very special goods.

Simplicity: The Amazon app offers its vendors, much like the client platform, because it's elegant and simple. Compared to many other e-commerce systems, it is much more effective and highly qualified. It is so much easier for you to operate with Amazon since you do not need to operate with several third-party systems like PayPal. You can even remove most of your tasks 9 out of 19 occasions such as registering the item, handling your charges, shipping item and taking pictures of high-quality goods. For you, Amazon works all in the business.

Visibility: tiny vendors find it more difficult to gain visibility on most e-retail sites for themselves and their products. You begin as a small portion of this enormous scheme, and it's really hard to get to the edge. Amazon is much superior to any other site for small vendors. Amazon utilizes a revolving search algorithm which from time to time maintains fresh vendors exposed to google outcomes for clients. You can even purchase supported connections if you can afford to ride far more visitors to your products and increase revenues. If you have a strong brand, you will create good profits.

Fee: The majority of individuals who operated in this company before a reasonable concept about the profits. They're narrow, are they not? That is the primary cause every vendor wishes his booking charges to be reduced. Again, Amazon is helping you and sparing your cash. On Amazon, for most items, you don't have to charge any booking charge. Certain unique kinds still need a booking charge, but opposed to other systems it's so minimal that you receive it happily. This enables you to maintain a versatile inventory, as you minimize initial expenses.

Facility to order: Most e-commerce platforms don't worry about how you can deliver your goods to clients and how your shipping demands are delivered on time. Amazon is distinct, and it's your own headache! Amazon may take care of and fulfill all your orders if you wish. You do not have to operate difficult to complete your commands or to keep relationships with fulfilling associates. Amazon is responsible for this and simplifies your work and makes the scheme work simpler.

Overhead Costs: In any company, overhead expenses are unavoidable, and every salesman seeks to minimize them. Amazon also appears as a seller's winner here. It enables in so many respects you reduce your overhead costs. You don't have to charge any registration fees or maintenance costs mostly to receive high-resolution photographs for your products. You even save time to communicate. This allows Amazon one of today's cheapest sites.

The prospect of growth: Amazon is a leader in e-retail, with its passion for technology and effectiveness, and will do so in the foreseeable future. Amazon will proceed to take a large portion of it and maximize your market exposure. The business is growing. You can develop in this location.

Integration: If you are among those who don't want to interact with a transaction supplier such as Paypal, market researchers such as TeraPeak or ShipWire and don't want to decide which instruments and sizes you would like to use, you should go to Amazon. You are not a payment provider. It streamlines and creates it simple for you to navigate without needing to create many difficult decisions. You are able to stop studying how to operate and handle everything from a single API through all these facilities. You are fully integrated with all manner of facilities and everything from your Amazon account can be monitored.

Stability: one of the most effective and stable devices for Amazon. It works efficiently and is not likely to change frequently, so it is not necessary every so often to go through a curve. There are many other devices that change their design and workflows solely to appear vibrant, but vendors can have an issue. There's no need to care about altering populations, marketplace laws, charges or characteristics, so Amazon is very stable.

Chapter 4: eBay

It has never been easier to conduct business online. Be it to earn some passive income or to create a business empire and stop being employed, eBay is the place to be. eBay is an online-based market place that provides a portal where millions of sellers globally have set up shop. They all depend on this platform to trade, make some good money and grow their businesses.

Benefits of Selling on eBay

There are many benefits that both you and your business will reap from using the eBay e-commerce platform. These benefits are:

1. You will have access to the global industry and millions of purchasers.
2. You can build your own store and a brand for your company.
3. You can readily find yourself on the search engine of eBay as soon as you have the correct name and rates, so you may not even have to sell your goods using other marketing and advertising strategies.
4. eBay offers security for sellers.

5. You can sell almost anything on eBay, so it can be simple to figure out what kinds of goods you want to sell online.

6. eBay provides you with a multitude of methods to tailor your listings.

7. eBay offers you unlimited possibilities to boost your revenue and expand your internet company.

8. eBay makes "testing the waters" convenient for you, allowing you to experiment with goods, rates and more.

9. eBay enables you to help well-known organizations while simultaneously selling goods.

For many company holders who want an easy manner to sell their goods, eBay is an excellent starting point, so why not jump on the eBay train and take your own eBay vendor trip? With this book, you can solve any doubt you feel about selling on eBay and also understand you can do it. If you are willing to know how to make cash on eBay, go to the next portion of this chapter.

Top 5 eBay Pre-Selling Tasks to Undertake

It is essential to prepare yourself for selling on eBay, particularly if you have zero indication of being a vendor. It's not an intelligent choice to jump into the eBay ocean without your life jacket. There are five activities you need to do to assist you to get ready for your eBay selling adventure, and they are outlined below:

1. Register for an eBay and PayPal account.

It's a no brainer to create an eBay account, but why PayPal? Since they are services produced by the same business, eBay and PayPal are linked. PayPal is the most common way to accept all eBay payments, so creating a PayPal account with an eBay seller account is important. First of all, let's go over how to sign up for PayPal by following these simple steps:

Registering for a Paypal Account

a. Go to PayPal.com and press on the top right corner of the "Sign Up" panel.

b. You will be transferred to a fresh site where you choose the sort of PayPal account you want to build: private or corporate. It is highly recommended that you go with a business account as it will render it simpler for clients to receive payments. Click "Continue" after selecting the Business choice.

c. You will be questioned which payment method you would like to use after selecting the account sort. Go with the Standard option (it's free!) as the other payment solutions are more appropriate for individual websites. You will be redirected to a website where you will start creating your account by filling out your private data forms.

d. Complete the first type and include your account's email address. Make sure that you write the code as well. Then press "Next." The complete form you need to fill out will be taken to you. Click "Accept and Continue" after reviewing PayPal strategies, and your business account will be set up. If you want to create a strong reputation as a vendor, you will also need to check your account. If you are a U.S. citizen, add your bank account data to check your PayPal account; in 2-3 days, PayPal will deposit a particular quantity of money you need to log in to your account's verification segment. You can find checking criteria for your country here if you are a global vendor. You may also need to verify your email address, so check your PayPal inbox for an official email.

You can readily upgrade it to a business account if you already have a PayPal account, but it's a private one. The steps by which your personal account is upgraded to a business account are:

a. Look for the hyperlinked word "upgrade," which should appear on the overview section of your account. You will be redirected to a website where you will find information about two kinds of account upgrades: corporate and first. Go with the choice for a business account.

b. Click the key "Upgrade Now" and select the sort of upgrade you want to receive. Make sure you go carefully through the upgrade process, then click "Continue." After that, your account should be upgraded to a business account.

Registering for an eBay Account

The next stage is to register for your eBay account after you have created your PayPal business account. Here are the instructions to do this:

a. Go to eBay.com and press "Register" at the main page's top-left corner.

b. Fill in the registration form. After reading the strategies and completing the document, press "Submit."

c. Now that you have logged into your account, you may see a "Start Selling" key. Click on it if you do. You can also locate a comparable key on the top left corner of the website; click on it, and you will go through the method of registering the Seller Account.

d. You can now get to the fun stuff and begin listing your products after signing up for a seller's account on eBay. At the bottom of the list, click on the "Sell" alternative (can be on the left or right side based on the section), and you will go directly to the item delivery method.

Link Your PayPal Account to Your eBay Account

After you have created both your eBay and PayPal accounts, you need to connect both to receive payments. Follow these simple steps to do this:

a. In the top menu bar, click on the My eBay tab.
b. Go to My eBay's "Account" folder: summary section.
c. Find and press on the "PayPal Account" option on the left sidebar.
d. Find the "Link My PayPal Account" option and log into your PayPal account to connect it to your eBay account. Well, all of you are ready to accept payments!

2. Do Your Research And Decide What To Sell.

The second step is to decide what you want to sell on eBay after having the tedious duties out of the way. You can collect any products in your house that you no longer want and are in excellent shape–making it more attractive to consumers–and list them on eBay to get your feet moist. For example, if you have vintage items you want to get rid of, check that they are in good condition and will not break or fall apart in any way after they arrive at the home of the buyer.

Starting with your home selling products can assist you to acquire expertise and build the reputation of your seller. You can then expand your stock and sell additional items. There are other ways to find products to offer if you don't have any items to sell in your home or you don't want to begin with this method:

i. *Find products you'd purchase and be interested in personally.*

One way to determine the products you are supposed to sell is to find one or more items that will flow your adrenaline and fly your spirits. In other words, find something you would love to sell and feel good about. Sell Disney movies (by the way, they're super popular!) if you love Disney movies. Selling kitchenware or cooking books if you sell cooking. Sell products you support; doing business like this is much more enjoyable.

ii. Go to the retail and thrift stores in the garage.

These two places are eBay sellers ' gold mines. In garage sales and thrift stores, as well as high-end products, you can discover rare vintage items at incredibly small rates. The main goal you have purchased to resell items is to create much more than you spent on the product. Therefore, cheaper yet useful products can dramatically increase your profits. Take a weekend off to discover garage sales in your area; you can even use internet tracker tools to locate nearby garage/yard stores like YardSaleSearch.com.

iii. Check the Popular Items List of eBay

This is another resource where you can find numerous famous products for sale on eBay in all categories, from antiques to jewelry; even mixed products can be found on this list, which enforces the fact that you can buy almost anything on eBay. To sell popular items, don't be intimidated. It's true that your market will have competitors, but it doesn't mean you can't create purchases or you have to reduce your rates to compete. Selling hot items is actually useful to you because you understand customers will want to buy them, which means more traffic and revenues for you.

iv. Sell products complementing bigger, more popular products

Electronics is one of eBay's high-selling items, so you can supplement them with products. Buyers like to have accessories with their touchscreen devices, for example, so why not offer stylish, durable covers to assist bring individuality and security to their devices? You don't have to concentrate on the "big" items; just as good are the accessories and "extras."

v. Sell your item of your own

If you've created an item that meets eBay policies, why not sell it and reach millions of consumers? Selling your own product provides you a distinctive edge against many vendors, and it also provides you the chance to create the credibility of your brand and product. You can also use eBay as your product's testing ground to see if it would perform well.

vi. Find inexpensive books on sales of novels

Book sales are U.S.-wide events hosted by non-profit organizations, and if you consider selling books on eBay, they're a gold mine for you. These book sale activities give comics at very low rates, but they are a first-come, first-serve ordeal; whoever receives the book first receives to purchase it, and they are attended by many online sellers. To help you get started with book sales, visit the website below to make it easier and faster for you to find book sales:

BookSalesFound.com–Become the only dealer with BookSalesFound.com at your next book sale! You're not going to have to wait until libraries add revenues to other databases. What is the difference between BookSalesFound.com and other websites? In order to provide you with a list of extremely lucrative book sales, we personally contact every library, nonprofit and auction house in the U.S. Most of the book sales on our list are exclusive, so with BookSalesFound.com, you will experience less competition. Sign up today for a free trial of 30 days.

vii.   Get from local shops or online retailers low-priced products

Retail arbitration is when you purchase a low-priced item or item that is sold in retail shops or online marketplaces and resell it at a greater cost for profit. But finding excellent deals on a multitude of products can be hard, so here's a wonderful resource you can use:

ScoutBotPro.com –Do you want to get information correct in your inbox about great deals on Amazon products? Every day, thousands of cheap, ready-to resell items are mentioned on Amazon, but you may not be able to go through them yourself. The tedious job is being performed for you with ScoutBotPro.com! Scout Bot Pro will notify you via email when an extremely low-priced item has been found on Amazon, making it simple for you to buy products for profit reselling. Register today for a free 30-day trial and see what ScoutBotPro.com has to offer for yourself.

Hopefully, you can find out the products you would like to sell on eBay from one or more of these tips.

3. Have you got your item? On eBay, double-check your potential achievement.

If you have a concept of what you want on eBay to sell, it's time to test and see if you've got a winning item. All this study can be done directly on eBay, so here are the measures to do this:

a. Go to eBay.com and enter your search bar element in the name. Try to make the search term as straightforward as feasible (2-3 letters). Also, make sure it's not wrong. I'm going to look for hair straighteners as an instance and pretend it's a feasible item I'd like to sell.

b. When the findings of the quest appear, go to the left sidebar. You will see tons of sophisticated search alternatives, but locate the section called "Show Only" close the bottom of the search choices list to see if an item will be effective. Under this chapter there will be three options: Accepted Returns, Completed Listings and Sold Listings.

c. Check the cabinet next to "Sold Listings" and automatically update the query outcomes to display you all product-related sold listings. On the first page, the latest sold ads begin. You will see green-colored prices on the right side of the search outcomes; this is an indication that a product has been effectively marketed. Here are a few examples of green-colored hair straighteners rates: as you can see, prices for products can differ greatly, but they can also be purchased at distinct rates, regardless of how large or low they are. Try not to get into the mindset that you're going to get more orders if you reduce your prices. Many customers believe in "greater cost, greater quality" conditions.

d. What do you do on the Sold Listings section now? Seller notoriety and feedback–note the percentage and read the buyers ' comments;

- How many items they have purchased if more than one item is accessible for purchase;
- How the vendor wrote their item description;
- If the vendor has clear, crisp item photos;
- If the vendor uses an effective item description;

Why are these elements looked at? You want to know if to create a successful sale they did something different compared to other vendors. Call this analysis of competitors or fundamental study–this is a significant move either way. You want to know this data so that attractive sites can be created to encourage individuals to buy products from you. But create sure you only do this process to collect information, not to copy listings from other sellers; this is not an ethical or professional technique.

4. Defines your sale objective on eBay.

Even if you want an extra $100 a month to be made, you always want to know what your objective is to begin selling on eBay. It will not only assist you to increase your likelihood of getting a successful eBay voyage, but it will also assist you to place yourself in the correct mindset.

Having no clue what your purpose is for anything in life isn't the correct way to go; you're only going to walk aimlessly, and that's going to create you look unprofessional and incompatible as a vendor on eBay. This is why determining your purpose for selling on eBay is critical.

Also, create sure your original eBay objective is realistic. Sure, there are tales out there where vendors can sell an object in an hour, but your product may not sell for a month or more at times. Do not concentrate on fast money; rather, decide on an objective that will ultimately not let you down and create you give up.

5. Set times for checking your eBay accounts throughout the day.

Set at least one time to check your eBay account for messages from potential buyers if you have even one product listed on eBay. You should also take the moment to see how your applications, such as how many opinions you have received so far, are doing.

If you want to create it simpler to see if you have any latest activity on your listings, you can receive email notifications whenever you receive an eBay message or your product has purchased a notification. You can read the updates directly from your email on your items. Go to your eBay account overview section by clicking on the top right corner of "My eBay." Then go to the "Account" tab and tap on "Communication Preferences." You'll be drawn to a page with multiple email notification choices, so go through each segment and inspect the notifications you want to obtain in your email inbox.

Checking your eBay account at least once a day will assist you to maintain your eBay activity better tracked. You don't take it seriously enough if you neglect it. It's interesting to start selling your own products and be your own boss, so if you have items mentioned, create every attempt to check your eBay account every day.

Now that you know what to do before selling on eBay, let's go on so that you can finally get those products listed and start making cash!

eBay Selling Essentials

You've built up your eBay vendor account and PayPal account, so it's time to learn about eBay selling basics. We will go through the different elements you need to know about when buying on eBay during this eBay trip.

Then we're going to get to the pleasant things–list your products and make cash! Once you are booked into your eBay selling account, the entire eBay universe is your playground and it's time to explore. This journey will demonstrate to you the main parts of your eBay selling trip, so let's start.

Where to go If you want to list a product

No matter which website you go to on eBay, at the bottom of the website there will always be a primary menu bar. One of the alternatives is called "Sell," and you want to tap on it whenever you want an item to be listed. Once you've started on that option, you're going to be redirected to a site that looks like this: I'll demonstrate to you how to list your products later on in this eBay trip, but you still need to understand where you can access the booking page immediately. That's why eBay sale is one of the essentials.

Feedback

On eBay, both customers and vendors have the chance to leave feedback and feedback helps to create credibility, regardless of whether you are a customer or vendor. If you see positive feedback on your profile, it also helps individuals trust you more. You always want to do your utmost as a seller on eBay to obtain positive feedback. The steps to do this are to access your input:

a. Hello, < your name >!"Top of the website menu option and hover over your cursor.

b. A drop-down menu will occur and you will see a star and the number of parentheses feedback you have. Click on the hyperlinked list and you'll achieve your "Feedback Profile." This is where you can see your overall feedback proportion, remarks and On your Feedback Profile, you'll also get a graph of complete favorable, neutral and negative input you've got over the past 1, 6 and 12 months.

This is an excellent instrument to verify frequently so you understand how you're doing overall as a seller. Go to the product the buyer has purchased to leave feedback. On the correct hand of the section, the product data is in, after clicking on the dropdown arrow, you will see a dropdown menu and a Leave Feedback option. Sometimes you can click on the Leave Feedback option, so you don't need to use the drop-down menu to use that intervention. Leaving feedback is a simple process where you rate your buyers and post your feedback profile for a short comment.

Your eBay Summary Page All you need to access is on the overview section of your eBay. This is where all your purchases will be found if you purchase products on eBay, information from the seller and other information. All you need to do to get to your eBay overview section is click on "My eBay" at the bottom right corner of the menu bar.

Your Seller's Summary Page

The summary page of the seller is an important instrument for every eBay seller to access all your accounts and other seller data. Just go to "My eBay" and press on the "Sell" alternative to get to it. When you reach the All Selling page, you will see various parts that connect to your knowledge of selling. For example, Monthly Selling Limits are the first part, and each vendor has a different limit. When you begin, eBay will give you a $5,000 or 100 product listing cap. In other words, you can list only items totaling $5,000 or less or listing 100 or fewer products.

Other parts you should understand about on the All Selling page are:

- **Active Selling**: This section demonstrates all of your active listings.

- **Sold**: This segment shows all lists sold and helps you handle shipping, feedback, etc.
- **Returns**: This segment shows all products returned.
- **Unsold**: This segment will go to this segment when the listing ends and has not been purchased. You can also manage, e.g. relist or delete the unsold items here.

Although not needed, on the overview section of the seller there is another section that you can maintain an eye on promotions. As a vendor, you get exclusive listing deals, such as freeing up the first 50 listings, so visit this section from moment to moment to see what kinds of advertising deals you are eligible for. The section on Promotional Offers is at the bottom of the page.

Selling Totals

You will discover a Totals segment on the left sidebar on the All Selling website. The information in this summary is:

- Current listings
- Selling listings (which are listings with buyers ' offers)
- Total offers for all listings

- Sold products
- Payments obtained and not obtained on products purchased.

The Totals segment is an excellent way to quickly and easily keep track of your sales advancement.

eBay Fees

Since eBay offers you a location to sell your products, charging charges is only reasonable to assist promote your selling journey, right? However, what you can do to compensate for the fee expenses is to include the expenses in your items ' rates. The eBay charges you should be aware of are:

Insertion Fee

The first 50 sites are free each month, but this may change depending on the category in which you shop. You will be paid an insertion charge of $0.05 for items in the fields of Books, DVDs & Movies, Music and Video Games and $0.30 for other applications after using your 50 free listings. You will be paid an insertion premium of $0.30 for all listings after 100 listings.

Final Value Fee

For all offers, an initial value fee is 10 percent of the buyer's total amount, which comprises the price of the product and the price of shipping.

Additional Listing Fee

eBay provides listing upgrades (e.g., daring font impacts and subtitles) and costs them a premium.

Reserve Price Fee

The eBay costs $2 for reserve rates between $0.01 and $199.99 if you put a specified price for your auction-styled listings. Reserve prices starting at $200 and up are charged at 1 percent, and the full premium is $50.

10-Day Auction Listing

You will be paid $0.40 if you decide to go with a 10-day auction listing.

Second Category Fee

You will be paid a payment for the second category if you select an additional category for your item.

Check out the eBay fee calculator to offer you the greatest estimate of your charges if you want to find out how much you are going to pay in charges. This calculator will also see how much charges you pay and help you generate plans for sale, so bookmark the website!

These must-know eBay sale basics were described in this chapter from the registration region to the eBay fees.

Hopefully, by reading through the sections so far, you have become used to being a seller on eBay!

eBay Selling

Listing Your Items

You understand the five essential elements of eBay selling and have experienced how to build an eBay and PayPal account, so now you're prepared to register and sell! How to create your listings is the next stop on this eBay trip. Listing your first product for sale is an exciting experience, so you want to create the listing ideal.

Depending on which products you intend to sell, the listing method differs slightly because certain items require specific details. I'm going to use Disney movies as an example to demonstrate the booking process. Let's start with it!

1. Click on the bottom of the eBay home page to "Sell." If needed, log into your eBay account.

2. In the space provided on the reservation board, type an item name. You can also enter a product's UPC, ISBN, VIN or other code. If eBay acknowledges the item name, a list of keywords and associated products will be displayed. To kick off your registration, you can choose one of these recommendations as your product name.

3. Click the "Start" button or press the Enter key and you will be redirected to the next part of the bidding method, which is to select a class for your item. You will automatically be redirected to the second portion if you select a keyword or suggested item from the drop-down menu. This is where you enter all the information you need about the product.

4. Double-check the correct category for your item and print the item title to render it search-friendly. To make it search-friendly, keywords that customers would search for must be in the item name. For the item name, you have 80 characters to use, so use the space wisely. Some effective product titles instances include:

    i. Cinderella Disney Movie DVD Blu-Ray 2-Disk Set

    ii. 16 oz. Clear Tumbler With Reusable Straw

iii. Red KitchenAid Stand Mixer 5-Quart Depending on the category you choose, a fee may be paid. eBay sometimes has free subtitles offers, so when you create your profile you will see the promotion.

The subtitle is a beneficial component of a listing because it gives you more room to include more information about your item and helps to increase your search opportunities.

5. Select the condition in which your item is after finishing the item title section. With the condition, always be frank! That's a customer service form, so don't try to hype up your product and label it "Brand New" if it doesn't.

6. Add pictures of your item and use all 12 rooms if possible. The more pictures you display of your product, the more likely you are going to sell.

7. If appropriate, the next section, Item Specifics, can be completed. This is where you will be able to include more detailed item information. If you do not have this part, it may be due to the classification under which you have chosen to place your item.

8. Next, fill in the text box and give your purchasers more details about your products and other data. For

example, the times you ship your products, like every Wednesday and Friday, can be included.

9. Another additional listing option is the Listing Designer where you can contribute a theme for an additional charge to your listing. To see how you want your folder to look, you can run around with the booking designer. A little ornamental flair is added to your registration by the Listing Designer so you can invest in it if you want to spice it up. Under the Listing Designer, you'll see a Visitor Counter choice, which will tell you how many individuals are visiting your listing. You can hide it, or you can choose to show it in a unique font style on your listing.

10.   Next, you will specify your item cost and what kind of listing you want to produce. There are two distinct formats accessible for listing, and they are:

   i. **Auction-Style**: This format for listing is set up so buyers can bid on the product. To kick off the auction, you put a starting cost. The listing format of the auction-style has a reserve price choice where a concealed minimum cost can be set. The purpose of a reserve price is to guarantee that an item receives the minimum quantity of cash.

ii. **Buy It Now:** This listing format allows the customer to buy the item immediately without having to offer or wait for an auction to end. You can also include a Buy It Now discount in an auction-style listing to allow buyers to buy the item immediately. The Buy It Now listing format has a "Best Offer" choice that also applies to the listing so concerned customers can send you a product offer and you can acknowledge it, dismiss it or create a counteroffer.

In most cases, eBay will recommend the best price for you to set on the format and price section, and this is the average price you sell for similar products. You can follow the proposal of pricing given to you by eBay, or you can set a cost with which you are most comfortable.

11. If you have more than one of the same item open for purchase, register the amount of the item after choosing on the submission format and cost. Then set the sale duration. If it's an auction list, you can have the auction going for a period of 10 days. The maximum listing for a Buy It Now is "Good' Til Canceled," a duration option that allows you to keep

listing indefinitely until the listing is canceled. You can also contribute to a charity and set a proportion of donations to be taken from your sale. This proportion is drawn from the product's complete selling cost.

12. Decide how the next section will fare, which will most probably be PayPal. Make sure you have the right PayPal email address and labeled the checkbox next to PayPal.

13. Setting the shipping service and price arrives next after determining your payment method. For shipping, offer a precise shipping estimate so that your customers are not overcharged. Choose the finest shipping choice for your listing, register the price or verify "Free Shipping" if you want it to be delivered and set the time for processing. If you want to sell shipments to consumers in your nation only or not to other countries, be sure to fill in the Excluded Shipping Locations form below the chapter on shipping information.

14. Set your policy on product returns. In a certain time period, you can choose not to acknowledge returns or acknowledge returns. Fair warning here: even if you decide not to accept transfers, your no-return policy may not be applicable if the product is not as described in the register. You can choose a

return of 14, 30 or 60 days as well as how you will offer the client a refund. The choices are:

- Only cashback
- Return or replacement money (buyer selects)
- Return or exchange money (buyer selects)

Return policy of 30 days is the most efficient as a suggestion because it helps to boost your revenues. When buying from you, buyers want to feel safe, and this is one of the ways to do that.

Feedback on eBay is extremely essential, and the best way to cope with an unhappy client who wishes to transfer a product is to offer to pay for the price of return shipping, regardless of the reason. But if the client simply changed their minds about the item and no longer wants it, then the buyer should pay for return shipping.

15. You will be told any charges you charge in the last segment of the registration process. Click "Continue" after all of you have completed the registration method. If you want to operate on the listing later, press "Save For Later."

16. If you click "Continue," you will be redirected to a review section with an evaluation of any charges you charge and sophisticated upgrades to the register.

The upgrades include a bold format and a subtitle for the name of the product. If you need to edit or display your listing, scroll down and choose which one best suits your requirements until you see those options. Click "List Your Item" if you're prepared to create your listing public. Click the hyperlink to your listing to see how it appears, or go to the All Selling section to verify your registration stats and more.

Give yourself a pat on the shoulder and a round of applause because your first register has just been created! Hopefully, without a scratch, you could get through the listing process. Be sure to verify your All Selling page as well as the booking activity, e.g. views and watches, frequently after generating your item listings. Watches are when your item is saved on their Watch List by potential buyers, and this gives you an idea of how many people want your item.

You now understand how to build your listings, and that's when the party really begins. You will learn valuable eBay selling tips and tricks in the next section that will assist you to succeed and become more skilled in eBay sales.

eBay Success Selling Tips

You're fitted with basic eBay selling knowledge, so it's time to get cracked and be the next success tale for eBay. You will learn how to overcharge your selling tactics in this section to attract more customers, get more sales, increase earnings, and create your credibility online.

Top tips and tricks for all aspects of eBay selling listings are at the center of eBay selling; without them, you wouldn't be able to offer or make money for your products.

That's why your listings are such a crucial element of eBay sales, so let's use these tips and tricks to enhance your listings:

1. Always bear in mind your buyer's accounts.

The most fundamental rule of a listing is to create it for the customer at all times. Think about it this way: what would you like to include in the listing if you were a buyer? Would you like responses to what questions? While creating your listings, ask yourself these questions.

2. Include the reservation price in terms of the listing

If you set an auction reserve price, indicate it in the section Product title or information listing. You can also use the part subtitles to let buyers know your item's reserve price. The reserve price is more for the seller than the customer, so by publicly displaying it in your register, help customers to guess the cost. Another recommendation is to give free shipping, if possible, to assist relieve the anxiety of your buyers.

3. Provide your listings with precise shipping expenses

Buyers aren't clueless; when the shipping expenses are too high, they understand. Calculating a precise or near estimate of shipping expenses is better for your reputation. Get a postal scale to do that, which you can discover at an extremely small cost straight on eBay. A postal scale is an excellent investment because you're going to understand how much to charge on your accounts for shipping, and you're not going to have to travel to the post office just to buy shipping tags.

You can enter this information in the handy shipping label creator of eBay with the weight of the boxed-up item and print a shipping label for the item right in your home. eBay also offers shipping calculators to vendors to assist with shipping expenses.

4. Get free crates from eBay for USPS shipping

This eBay resource is ideal for you if you're a U.S. vendor, particularly if you're planning to sell bigger products. You can order free packages from eBay's catalog and have them shipped to your house. Do not mistake this resource, however, like free shipping. You only get free shipping materials; you need to buy the real shipping label.

5. Determine the correct auction listing length

eBay provides auction durations of 1-, 3-, 5-, 7-and 10-day durations. One of these length moments is ideal for it, depending on your product. For example, for high-selling products, 1-day auctions are best because bidders will jump at the chance to get them at a fantastic price. Also, on the search engine of eBay, 1-day auctions will get you noticed more if customers are looking for auctions that will quickly end.

To offer you a clearer concept of which auction performs best for your products, here is a mini overview of the other duration periods:

a. **3-day:** This time interval for an auction is comparable to a 1-day auction, but it gives customers more time to think about buying the product or not. Three-day auctions are also best suited to high-selling products. It is fine to give a Buy It Now discount for both 1-and 3-day auctions so buyers can buy the product instantly.

b. **5-day**: If you begin your auction on Wednesday and want to stretch it over the weekend, the easiest route to go is through a 5-day auction, particularly for hot-selling products. This gives shoppers the opportunity to bet on your product at the weekend.

c. **7-day**: Auctions over the course of the week give you the opportunity to reach more customers. Online shoppers also have a week-long opportunity to bet on your product.

d. **10-day**: Ten-day auctions are best for costly items and collectibles as it gives more time for buyers to locate their listing, particularly if you start on Friday. With a 10-day auction, you will cover two weekends. Use the 10-day auction option for top-selling products as a suggestion. Short-term auction periods are easier because for bidders they are more interesting.

6. *Properly Time your Post Listing*

To publish your listing, choose the best time. Your listing starts and ends at the same time, regardless of your choice of day or duration. Sunday night is the most popular ending day agreed by most sellers, preferably finishing at 8-9 p.m. PST, so attempt listing your items at the moment to finish. It is understandable that you want to register your products as quickly as you can and make money as soon as possible, but eBay is not just a platform for listing and selling. You are a seller now, and to reap the most benefits, it is essential to understand how to sell tactics and approaches. If you want to get out of the way websites, go through the creation procedure for booking and save it for later. You can also use a free eBay tool to plan your deals: Turbo Lister.

7. *Avoid using your listings with brand names*

Chanel, for example, is a brand name that causes a ton of individuals in eBay trouble. Keyword spamming and copyright violations are considered to include it in your register, so prevent using brand names in your item name and listings. Even if you see other sellers in their listings using brand names, that doesn't imply it's permitted.

8. Before you make it live, check your listing

On any of your listings you don't want to create a mistake, so make sure you have zero spelling, grammar, and punctuation mistakes. It will create you look more professional by reviewing and revising your listings.

9. Create your batch listings

It's no secret that listing is a tedious job and takes a ton of time to create, but there's an easier way to handle the listing process. Batch comparable assignments together instead of generating one listing at a moment. Here's an example task list for batching:

- Take 7-10 pictures of each product.
- Come up with product titles for each product and enter them in a spreadsheet.
- Set the prices for each item and enter the prices in the spreadsheet.
- Determine which listings are auction-style and Buy It Now on the spreadsheet (e.g. make an Auction or Buy It Now?" column".
- Figure out the shipping costs for each product and enter the costs in the spreadsheet.
- Write the product details for each listing directly in the spreadsheet or copy and paste it in the spreadsheet.

Completing similar tasks together will help you keep the flow going, and it'll also help you get these steps done faster. You can use a spreadsheet or a document to keep track of all your listing information.

10. Avoid using negative terms in your Listings

Saying things such as "I am not responsible for lost or stolen packages" or "Don't bid if you are not planning to pay" on your listings will drive buyers away; they don't want to deal with a seller who seems rude and unapproachable. Just let buyers know to contact you on eBay if they have questions.

The Right Price

Pricing is one of the biggest obstacles every eBay seller has difficulty overcoming, but there's no need to worry about it. With these pricing tips, you can place accurate and profitable prices on your items with ease.

a. If you're purchasing wholesale goods, make sure that you can double the price. Buying products in bulk is cheaper and can increase your profits when you resell them; however, in some cases, you may not make a decent amount of money because your product is too expensive compared to other similar products on the market. To ensure that you can double the price on the product and sell it easily, check eBay's Sold Listings section in search when you look up products similar to yours and look at the prices. Can you comfortably sell the product in your category? If not, figure out other ways that you can double the price, such as pairing the item with a complimentary item. For example, if you plan to sell electronic tablet covers, offer them in pairs by color, such as blue and purple. Let the buyers know that they can switch up the covers to match their outfit or whenever they want to change the style of their tablet.

b. If you have a very popular product and want to put the product up for an auction, go with a low starting price. Low starting prices will help encourage bidders to place higher bids. Also, with all the eBay snipers on the watch, people are more likely to spend more on a product because they're thinking about winning the auction instead of the cost. If you have an incredibly popular or rare item, setting a low starting price is a great way to increase your profits. If you want to be on the safe side, apply a reserve price on the listing.

c. Use the "What's It Worth?" feature on eBay. This feature is linked to a program called Terapeak, which offers a 7-day free trial for sellers. Terapeak gives you the ability to place competitive prices on your items as well as help improve your pricing and selling strategies. If you plan to sell long-term or grow a business on eBay, Terapeak is a worthwhile investment since you'll get exclusive information that's not available publicly, increase your profits and enhance your selling experience.

d. Consider your shipping charges. When sellers have an expensive item listed for sale, the one selling tactic they use is offering free shipping. If you plan to sell products that cost $100 or more, provide free shipping if you're comfortable enough with that idea. It'll help increase your chances of getting purchases or bids. You can include the shipping fee in the product price itself, but buyers will know if the product price includes the shipping fee or not. Some sellers include the shipping fees in the price, and some eat the cost. It's up to you how you want to handle free shipping. Another selling method to include shipping is to charge half the shipping fee in the actual shipping costs section and add the other half to the product price.

Customer Service

From restaurants to clothing stores, customer service is present in all businesses. Even if you're selling on eBay as a hobby, you have to maintain excellent customer service. You're selling products to other people for money, so that is still considered a business exchange or trade. Customer service is also what makes or breaks a seller's reputation, so don't let your customer service slip. Here are a few tips to help you deliver outstanding customer service:

a. Listen to your customers

If your customers have sent you questions about any of your items on eBay, read their messages thoroughly and understand what they're asking about. Then, answer their questions or concerns honestly. Honesty is the best policy after all! Customers will notice if you're paying attention to their message or not, so be sure to not rush through the message.

b. Deal with negative feedback professionally

It's no fun getting negative –even neutral –feedback, but you may run across a buyer who's not too happy. First off, don't sweat it, and don't retaliate. Nothing good comes out of an argument with a buyer. If you get negative feedback, you can either reply to the feedback or message the buyer. Ask them if there's anything that you can do to rectify the situation. If the buyer doesn't respond after a week, let it go. Don't let one negative feedback put you down. This will also show other buyers that you're a considerate and professional seller, so don't worry about 1-2 negative or neutral comments.

c. Take time to give your buyers feedback

You don't have to write a specific comment for every buyer; most sellers actually have a set of feedback ready for them to post, and that's what you can do as well. Create a few general comments that you can copy and paste into the feedback section for the buyer. You don't have to get fancy with it. Also, don't wait until you've received feedback from the buyer to leave feedback. If the buyer has already purchased and paid for the product, give them feedback right away; they've already done their part.

d. Add a small "thank you" note to packages

Express your gratitude to your buyers by including a "thank you" note to their package. You can use a simple sticky note or slip of paper to write a short "thank you" note, such as this one: Hi Susan, Thank you very much for your purchase! Enjoy, -Frank Keep it short and simple.

e. If time allows you, answer all messages promptly

It may not be possible to do so when you have other responsibilities to take care of, but answering customer messages in a timely fashion will boost your customer service reputation. Most buyers on eBay are impulsive buyers, so answering messages quickly will increase your chances of someone purchasing your product.

f. Offer shipping discounts

If a buyer is interested in purchasing multiple products, but they don't want to pay all the separate shipping prices, you can offer them a shipping discount for buying multiple products. Depending on what shipping service you use, you can squeeze in several products in one box for a flat rate, such as USPS Priority Mailboxes. What you can do is calculate the total shipping costs for all the items the buyer wants and add the total costs of the items to the shipping costs. Then, create an invoice in PayPal with the total amount (shipping + product costs) and send it to the buyer.

The steps to do this are to produce an invoice in PayPal:

1. Log in and click on the "Request Money" panel to your PayPal account.

2. Click "Create Invoice," and to produce your invoice you will be given to a website.

3. To send your invoice, fill in the required documents. First, include the email address of the recipient on the left side, under the "Send To" segment. Check your "Business Information" segment to ensure that your data is accurate. You can leave the section "Invoice Information" as it is, so you don't have to think about it.

4. Complete the item form in the next chapter. This is where the multiple products the customer wishes will be listed along with the cost for each product. How to add more rooms to display all item information is the "+" sign on the far right hand. The standard type has only one object room.

5. Include, if needed, a notice and conditions. Then register the quantity of shipment and processing. If you do not pay tax on your products or are not eligible to do so, hold the choice "No Tax" for any tax-related segment.

6. Scroll down the document and click the "Send" button in yellow-orange.

7. It was supposed to have sent your invoice, so the buyer's notification about the invoice. Wait until the purchaser sends you the money before shipping the goods. That's everything you need to do!

Another method is to generate a unique, customized purchaser register. Include the complete registration expenses and send the connection to the file to the purchaser. Let them buy through that listing their items. Be sure to include in the product name or subtitle something like "Custom Listing for Susan B." or "Custom Listing Do Not Buy" to avoid confusion with other consumers.

Organization for an eBay Seller

Selling on eBay is thrilling and you want to get your listings up and running as quickly as feasible and get those "Your item sold!" The eBay emails. But don't make the mistake of rushing into this, or you're only going to suffer major consequences you might have avoided at the start. Check out these helpful tips to assist you to get organized and build your own eBay seller room at home:

1. Designate a region of your house as your "office room." Packaging materials, a printer, a laptop,

your products and anything else you need should have a designated room in your house, such as a garage or a spare room. This is the basis for the successful sale of your eBay. When you get a sale, you don't want to scratch around attempting to locate a bubble mailer.

2. Do not transport on a daily basis. Anyway, who likes to drive every day to the post office? Choose from 1-3 days of the week instead of drop off your supplies at the post office. By doing so, you're saving gas time and cash. If they have that service accessible, you can also plan pick-ups with your post office at home. This service is available to USPS, and you can plan one on their website. For cheaper, handy tags, you can also use the shipping label service from eBay.

3. Keep track of all your income and expenses. Use an easy table to keep track of your income and expenses, such as eBay transaction charges.

Keeping up with trends

This is important as changes happen quicker in today's trends, and your item may be "in" for now, but what about next month or next year? It can be hard to sell the same product types on eBay unless you offer something like Disney movies that is timeless.

Otherwise, don't make your item too comfortable yet. You need to sharpen your competitive edge if you want to remain in the eBay match. To maintain track of trends and changes, here are several areas you can search for fresh patterns and product ideas:

a. **eBay's top-selling products:** In this section, you can discover the products most marketed on eBay that can give you an understanding of what products to offer.

b. **Newspapers and magazines**: From celebrities to fashion, gold mines are newspapers and magazines for trend information.

c. **Television**: Commercials and displays may be the key to your new item on eBay.

d. **Radio**: Listen to popular radio shows and see what is popular in today's culture, particularly in music. In this ocean of MP3 players and iPods, CDs are still in fashion!

How to Increase Your eBay Profits

Once you begin to see cash flowing in from your eBay revenues, the willingness to produce more is natural. eBay offers you countless opportunities to increase your sales and earnings, including several ideas:

Expand

eBay has a "sister" website called Half.com, a media product selling platform such as films, books, textbooks, and matches. Do not restrict yourself to eBay if you are interested in selling your ancient films and games or popular books. Half.com is another excellent location to make more products available and gain more money.

Sell products from the season

Christmas is a great holiday season as everybody tries to find the perfect last-minute gifts wherever they can and other holidays. Take advantage of these periods of shopping and offer seasonal products or products that people would like to give as presents, such as jewelry, clothing, stuffed animals and other accessories.

Offer goods to overseas buyers.

International shipping can help you raise your income. Say you live in the U.S. where you have access to tons of brand names that are not available to many international buyers–that's the value right there, and many international buyers will pay any amount to get products that aren't available. That's not saying that you should charge a ridiculous amount of money; it means that when it comes to selling to international buyers, you don't have to worry about high shipping costs if you have them.

Conclusion

Thank you for making it through to the end of dropshipping, let's hope it was informative and able to provide you with all of the tools you need to achieve your goals whatever they may be. From the topics covered in this book, it is now possible for you:

> Adequately prepare for your business venture by first conducting a self-analysis and determining which areas or departments of the business you may need some extra help.

> Properly prepare yourself for your next business venture in terms of market, product and supplier sourcing. These are the key elements that are vital to the survival of your business.

> Have the proper knowledge to open and run a professional Shopify, eBay or Amazon store.

> You understand the importance of search engine optimization and web traffic and will give it the necessary attention to ensure that your business has the right kind of visibility.

> You will be able to execute a proper marketing strategy, bearing in mind whether you will conduct

either a brand-oriented or a product-oriented campaign.

➢ You have the knowledge of the importance of leveraging your business success in a bid to take it to greater heights, and not just enjoying it and the profits that come along with it.

The next step now is to go out there and begin working on making your dreams a reality. With most (if not all) of the misconceptions have been clarified, you are now in a better position to start and run your own business than you were before you began reading this book. Finally, if you found this book useful in any way, a review on Amazon is always appreciated!

Description

Are you feeling stuck in your current workplace and want to challenge yourself a bit more? Or has your business hit a rough patch and you are looking for ideas and ways in which you can get it making money for you again? Well, the fact that you are reading this means you are one step closer to getting the answers that no one has been willing to answer for you.

In this era we are living in, running a part-time business is quite a simple venture. We no longer live in the times when planning to launch a business needs to be backed by a fat bank account to cater to your set up costs including inventory and warehousing. In most cases, all you need is a computer, smartphone or any other internet-enabled device and of course, a stable internet connection and you will literally be a single click away from beginning your journey to becoming an online business entrepreneur.

Even if you have a stable full-time job, in this economy it is always the smarter choice to secure for yourself a secondary income. This is because in case anything happens to mess around with your main source of income, your secondary income will help maintain your current lifestyle until you manage to get back on your feet again.

Dropshipping is the next best thing to hit the internet since the internet itself if I might say! Dropshipping is a method of doing business without ever having to manufacture a single product or even storing any stock. All you need to do is to set up an e-commerce store market, cater to customer requests and the rest of the processes are basically automated. In this book, you will get to learn:

➢ The things to do before you embark on the online business venture. You will get to learn of the things you will need to do and factors to consider before you embark on starting up your own business. Starting up a business online can be very simple and straight forward if you have the right information and tools but if you do not, it can be one vicious jungle.

➢ We will have a look at the best way to come up with the right marketing strategy for your product and brand. Once your online store is live and running, you will need to make it visible so that it can start getting customers who will bring in the money. The right marketing strategy will ensure you market your product to the right customer base and this is how you will make money.

➢ You will learn how to open a dropshipping store using the biggest popular and global champions in their respective fields in the e-commerce world. These three platforms are Shopify, Amazon, and eBay. You will get to learn how to create and set up your online store professionally in the respective platforms and how to get your business running in less than 12 hours.

➢ You will get to learn the importance of website traffic and search engine optimization (SEO) and how it directly affects the level of profitability for your business.